RAISING THE BAR

DIVERSIFYING BIG LAW

Debo P. Adegbile, Lisa Davis,
Damaris Hernández, and Ted Wells

As well as a conversation with leading
diversity professionals from top law firms

Edited with an introduction
by Anthony C. Thompson

*Published in conjunction with
the New York University School of Law
Center on Race, Inequality, and the Law*

THE
NEW
PRESS®

NEW YORK
LONDON

Published in the United States by The New Press, New York, 2019
Distributed by Two Rivers Distribution

ISBN 978-1-62097-496-4 (hc)
ISBN 978-1-62097-497-1 (ebook)
CIP data is available.

The New Press publishes books that promote and enrich public discussion and understanding of the issues vital to our democracy and to a more equitable world. These books are made possible by the enthusiasm of our readers; the support of a committed group of donors, large and small; the collaboration of our many partners in the independent media and the not-for-profit sector; booksellers, who often hand-sell New Press books; librarians; and above all by our authors.

www.thenewpress.com

Book design and composition by Bookbright Media
This book was set in Century Schoolbook and Copperplate

Printed in the United States of America

10 9 8 7 6 5 4 3 2 1

Contents

INTRODUCTION

DIVERSITY AND INCLUSION HAVE BECOME BUZZWORDS that organizations like to advance but too often have difficulty implementing. That is because embracing diversity and inclusion is fundamentally disruptive: it challenges the status quo and insists that organizations broaden their perspectives beyond what has gotten them to their current position. Embracing diversity and inclusion takes both leadership and courage. When we speak of leadership, we often imagine a superhero who leads us through a crisis. But the leadership that diversity and inclusion demand is the willingness to step up and admit that leaders come from different backgrounds, come in different hues, bring a different set of experiences and expectations. It is the courage to accept that those who have power and authority need to learn to share it, as well as learn from the perhaps unexpected sources of wisdom that distinguish today's leaders.

Often when people speak of leaders, they focus on elected officials, industry leaders, or public sector leaders who have captured the public's eye or attention. They are typically not thinking that any single profession is producing those leaders. But the fact is, many of the key leadership roles around the globe are held by people trained as lawyers. In this country alone, roughly half of the forty-five U.S. presidents have been legally trained. The U.S. Congress boasts over two hundred lawyers. Almost half of this country's governors are lawyers. Ten percent of the chief executive officers in the Fortune 500 companies are lawyers. When we drill down to include mayors, city council members, county commissioners, and those who lead domestic and global nonprofits, we again see an overrepresentation of attorneys. Boards of directors, advisory groups, and think tanks are also often led by lawyers. The influence that lawyers wield is unparalleled.

In many instances, those lawyers began their careers in law firms. This is not surprising. Large law firms play a critical role in today's world. They look to tackle many of the most challenging legal issues facing businesses, government, nonprofits, and individuals in an increasing complex and volatile world. There is perhaps an even greater urgency today for a more robust leadership role for lawyers in the nation and in the world. In particular, as tensions around social justice and racial equity continue to rise in the United States, and as politics cleave the country into opposing groups, there will be a growing need for substantial and sustained contributions from the private sector to help reset the moral compass and repair the social fabric.

Indeed, these volatile times call for lawyers of good

conscience to step up as leaders. But doing so requires not just performing conventional roles in the law and remaining relevant at critical junctures; lawyers and their firms need to take bolder steps to address issues of diversity and inclusion. Firms typically measure their success by their ability to be their clients' first choice when those clients need advice and expertise at the highest levels. Not surprisingly, firms routinely tout their intellectual agility, commercial acumen, and legal expertise as central to their brand, their competitive advantage, and the value that clients can expect they will provide. But what large law firms still need to recognize—and too often miss—is that their ability to foster and sustain a diverse and inclusive organization is also a key indicator of their value and an important predictor of their success.

Most law firms publicly commit to diversity and inclusion as guiding principles for their practices and policies. That is, of course, a good start. The problem lies in the failed execution of that normative assertion. There is a sizable chasm between the stated commitment and what actually occurs in practice. One reason for that gap may be that law firms tend to perceive diversity as simply a "good thing" to do rather than as a crucial driver of business and practice. Until law firms acknowledge that being diverse and inclusive helps their businesses thrive, they will continue to fall short of their diversity goals and ambitions.

The business case for diversity is clear. In its groundbreaking 2015 study, *Why Diversity Matters*, McKinsey & Company examined proprietary data sets for 366 public companies across a range of industries in Canada, Latin America, the United Kingdom, and the United States.* The researchers concluded that companies in the top quartile for gender, racial, and ethnic diversity were more successful financially. McKinsey has recently updated its research and expanded its data set to more than a thousand companies covering twelve countries. Its latest research confirms the continuous, global prevalence of the

---

* Vivian Hunt, Dennis Layton, and Sara Prince, *Why Diversity Matters*, McKinsey & Company, February 2015.

link between the diversity in companies' leadership (in terms of race, ethnicity, culture, and gender) and their ability to financially outperform other companies. In 2017, companies in the top quartile for ethnic and cultural diversity were 33 percent more likely to experience above-average profitability, and those in the top quartile for gender diversity were 21 percent more likely to outperform their peers.* Still, despite the compelling business case that these figures make, firm leadership overwhelmingly lacks diversity.

The lack of diversity among firms, both at the top and throughout their practice, has consequences. The clients that law firms hope to attract and retain are becoming more sophisticated and demanding in their expectations. Clients are more frequently insisting that the organizations they hire assign high-performing, diverse teams to help them anticipate and address the complex problems they face. If law firms continue to behave as they have—hiring

---

* Vivian Hunt et al., *Delivering Through Diversity*, McKinsey & Company, January 2018.

and promoting in their own image—they will find that their offices are dangerously homogenous, lacking the agility that a diversity of perspectives can produce and that clients expect. In an increasingly competitive and fast-paced environment, companies want legal counsel who can help them see around corners, identify trends and potential problems, and advise them how to navigate different environments and regulatory regimes. Firms that are diverse and inclusive can do just that, positioning their legal teams to serve as the trusted advisers that clients seek for the long term.

But issues of race and inequality continue to confound the legal profession. Law firms persistently face profound challenges in the recruitment, retention, and promotion of lawyers of color. Associates of color at law firms across the country continue to face obstacles in finding role models, mentors, and sponsors, and in experiencing the kind of job satisfaction that enables them to advance to positions of leadership within the firm. Law students from diverse backgrounds have little or no institutional guidance in choosing the right law firm or in understanding what it takes to become a vital member of their firm so they are positioned to receive the appropriate professional development as a young lawyer.

————————

To address this issue, the Center on Race, Inequality, and the Law at New York University School of Law brought together a spectacular group of law firm partners of color to engage in a robust and frank discussion about how law firms, associates, and law students can create more meaningful pathways to success for lawyers of color. The participants in that conversation were Lisa Davis, a partner at Frankfurt Kurnit Klein & Selz and one of the leading entertainment lawyers in the country; Debo P. Adegbile, a partner at Wilmer Cutler Pickering Hale and Dorr steeped in civil rights, litigation, and public service; Damaris Hernández, the first Latinx partner at Cravath, Swaine & Moore, widely recognized as a rising litigation star; and Ted Wells, co-chair of the litigation department at Paul, Weiss,

Rifkind, Wharton & Garrison, the honorary dean of the litigation bar, and a champion for the less fortunate. All of our panelists came to the conversation with a set of unique perspectives and a willingness to share their stories, which enriched both the discussion and our understanding of the chronic challenges regarding diversity in law firms. As the founding faculty director of the Center on Race, Inequality, and the Law, I have been concerned about the lack of diversity in the legal profession for some time. This program gave the center an opportunity to use our unique voice and vantage point to move this discussion forward, and articulate concrete steps that law firms, lawyers, and law schools can take to address this stubbornly persistent issue. In moderating and facilitating this conversation, I wanted to draw on the experiences, knowledge and commitment of these legal professionals, whose work on the ground offers critical insights into both the challenges and opportunities around diversity in big law.

The partner roundtable surfaced a number of pressing issues and prompted the Center to delve deeper, so next we convened a number of leading law firm diversity professionals to look even more closely at practices involving diversity and inclusion within law firms. We were fortunate to be able to host a conversation featuring Kiisha Morrow of Cravath, Swaine & Moore, Rachel V. Simmonds-Watson of Debevoise & Plimpton, Maja Hazell of White & Case, and Danyale A. Price of Paul, Weiss, Rifkind, Wharton & Garrison. We selected these participants because we believed them to be among the best diversity professionals in the country engaged in this important work. To jump-start the conversation, we asked, "What steps do we need to take to diversify law firms?" With that as our framing question, we invited the coordinators to help us examine best practices for the recruitment, retention, and promotion of associates of color in law firms. As with the law firm partners, the coordinators had unique insights about their experiences. What became clear is that partners, associates, and even law schools have their own important roles to play in enhancing and sustaining a diverse workforce in law firms. Perhaps the biggest contribution of the diversity professionals was their consensus view that firm partners, associates, and law schools were all in need of a "playbook" to help them address the challenges law firms face in developing more diverse offices. That insight led to the third section of this volume: the Playbook.

The Playbook addresses each of these audiences in turn. As the Playbook discusses in detail, partners, as they develop their own practice and book of business, must actively commit to diversity goals. That commitment is not satisfied by publishing a diversity statement or hiring a diversity professional. All partners must make a personal commitment to diversity much as they commit to other strategic and business goals. At large law firms in particular, the obligation to drive diversity initiatives often falls on partners of color and senior associates of color, creating a dual burden for these attorneys to succeed under traditional firm metrics while at the same time leading these crucial efforts. But diversifying the leadership ranks of law firms must be the responsibility of the entire firm's leadership. Firms need to identify ways to embed diversity goals into compensation structures and promotion criteria to begin to make their cultures more inclusive. But we cannot ask either white partners or partners of color to engage in this work without training. As with any task in this field, we need to prepare, train, and demonstrate the ways that individuals can effectively work on issues across difference.

All associates in law firms have a vital role to play in addressing issues of diversity as well. As the Playbook notes, white associates often serve as supervisors to junior associates and summer associates. When they are supervising someone of a different racial or ethnic background, it is important for white associates to take the time to understand that people of color may experience the firm differently. Too often, we tend to generalize from our own experience and assume that our personal perspectives represent the norm. But a commitment to diversity and inclusion means that white lawyers need to acknowledge the limitations of their own understanding and be willing to step outside of their personal experience to learn about and appreciate different experiences. At a minimum, white associates need to be alert to the challenges that people of color encounter simply by making up the minority in the firm, and need to take into consideration that early career associates of color may not feel as welcome at firm events or as comfortable with firm traditions. That awareness can serve as a starting point for white associates in being an ally and shaping a more inclusive culture.

Associates of color bear some personal responsibility in taking steps to ensure their own success in a law firm environment. They need to be aware that race still figures centrally in how they are perceived in law firms. Because of increasingly segregated housing, educational, and cultural patterns in the United States, white Americans often lack genuine knowledge and understanding of communities of color. The result is that stereotypes, fear, and suspicion continue to animate perceptions of lawyers of color. New lawyers of color need to be aware that those biases may influence—sometimes implicitly—opinions about their abilities as lawyers. Those biases may also lead white supervising attorneys to judge more harshly the mistakes made by associates of color, misconstruing normal developmental errors as evidence of something more problematic. As a way to combat these biases, lawyers of color and summer associates may need to be more engaged in seeking out mentors and raising their hands for assignments to get the opportunities that might come more easily to their white colleagues. Just as importantly, they need to understand that once they have entered the firm, the value proposition for success shifts. What got firms to hire them—their academic ability and intellect—are now just table stakes. They will need to do more to prove themselves in order to advance in the firm. They will need to develop a personal brand that will affect and shape their trajectory. Building that brand begins with their first experiences as a summer associate or entry-level lawyer. Even if lawyers of color do not intend to remain at a particular firm or to become a partner there, the early impressions they make within the firm will influence their ability to be successful in the law firm environment.

Last in order but not in importance, law schools have a crucial role to play in diversifying the profession. As the Playbook explains, law schools need to do more to prepare law students of color for the experience of working in a large law firm, including offering guidance in professional development and personal branding. To date, however, law schools have largely absented themselves from this process. Right now, they focus heavily on their placement statistics. Being able to demonstrate, for the purposes of national rankings, that their law students are hired by the top law firms is what helps them maintain a competitive advantage. But law schools need to pay attention not only to their front-end placement but also to the actual success of their graduates in these environments. That means law schools must determine what factors enable law graduates to thrive and rise within firms, and then share that information with students prior to their first summer associate experience. For law students of color, that training should also include instruction on how to navigate diversity challenges within law firms.

Similarly, law schools have a responsibility to ensure that white law students understand and appreciate the value of diversity and inclusion. Law schools often lack a diverse placement staff or the cultural competence to provide meaningful programming for Asian, African American, and Latinx students and alumni. In those institutions where that is the case, they must reach out and acquire that expertise. Deans of law schools need to have this on their radar if we are to truly make a difference in the ranks of private practice.

The conversations presented here demonstrate that the diversity challenge facing law firms is multifaceted and that several actors—firm leaders, associates and partners of color, law firm diversity professionals, and law school placement officials—must work in tandem to change the landscape and make law firm cultures more inclusive. Our hope is that the discussions, analysis, and recommendations in this book will spark conversations in law firms, bar associations, and law schools that will serve as a blueprint for improved diversity and help to raise the bar in the partnership ranks of our nation's law firms.

Race, Inequality, and the Legal Profession

A Public Conversation on Private Practice

The following section derives from a conversation with Anthony C. Thompson, New York University School of Law; Debo P. Adegbile, Wilmer Cutler Pickering Hale and Dorr; Lisa Davis, Frankfurt Kurnit Klein & Selz; Damaris Hernández of Cravath, Swaine & Moore; and Ted Wells of Paul, Weiss, Rifkind, Wharton & Garrison.

Tony Thompson: The issues of race and inequality have always been salient, but they've become much more salient today. We've watched as the national conversation has deteriorated into toxic tweets and finger-pointing. And the public debates on issues of racial and social justice reveal rising levels of misunderstanding, distrust, and division.

The challenge facing this generation is to draw a line in the sand with respect to inclusion, social justice, and racial, social, and gender equity.

I think it's very important to understand that the legal profession has always suffered from an inability to appreciate and value difference. Whether we're talking about the public sector or the private sector, our profession has not benefited from the rich racial and ethnic diversity of our communities and our country.

We've seen some moderate progress in the last decade, in part because we had someone in the White House for eight years who was good on issues of racial and social justice. The Obama administration took principled positions including reducing racial disparities in the criminal justice system, preventing states from erecting barriers to dilute the voting power of people of color, and prioritizing employment to bolster fairness. But the current administration is running to the past. It isn't looking to tear down the things that divide us; it's looking to build walls and incite hatred. It's placed an imprimatur on division, distrust, and fear.

When leadership in Washington fails, as it has on social and racial justice, we need to fill that void. We need to look to state and local government to step up. We need to look to individual citizens to say no to the government's excesses. And we need to look to the private sector to help restore the sanity of the nation's leadership.

Here with us, we have four superstars. They're from the private sector, but they've spent much of their professional lives serving in the public interest. And we'll have an opportunity to engage all four of them in a conversation about the profession, the nation, and leadership.

Damaris Hernández is a graduate of NYU Law School and the first Latina partner at Cravath, Swaine & Moore. In the twenty-plus years I've been on this faculty, she is one of the superstars that we've graduated, and I've seen her grow from a smart, strong young lawyer to a formidable partner in this city. Lisa Davis was a law review editor and a Root-Tilden scholar who went on to clerk for the honorable Constance Baker Motley. Lisa has worked at the epicenter of culture, politics, race, and gender. She's been identified as one of the best entertainment lawyers in America and has represented a broad range of clients, from the Pulitzer Prize–winning scholar Dr. Manning Marable to the rap group Public Enemy. Debo Adegbile, now a partner at WilmerHale, is a former NAACP Legal Defense Fund lawyer, a former senior counsel to the Senate Judiciary Committee, a seasoned Supreme Court litigator, and a champion of the rights of the disenfranchised.

And finally, we have Ted Wells. Long before I came to NYU over twenty years ago, when I was a trial lawyer in Northern California, I'd heard of Ted Wells. He is the dean, the heart and the soul of the bar. I don't engage in hyperbole when I say that Ted Wells is a lawyer's lawyer. He's represented, or at least been asked to represent, practically every high-profile client in the country, from elected and throughout much of the United States, and the DC school system was legally segregated. The Supreme Court decided *Brown v. Board of Education* in 1954, and I started kindergarten in September of 1955, right after the DC school system was desegregated.

A lot of people don't realize that Washington, DC, was one of the five school systems involved in *Brown*. From the perspective of my life, *Brown* was a critical event. It was the first time the Supreme Court overruled the "separate but equal" doctrine of *Plessy v. Ferguson* and took the position that America should have an integrated society, even though the Court qualified its mandate with "all deliberate speed." Nevertheless, I see real progress beginning with the *Brown* decision.

Derrick's view was similar to that. He used to say to me all the time: "Ted, we're not going to do this in your lifetime." If you have that perspective—that America just began to try to overcome its racial inequities with the *Brown*

appointed officials to organizations and law firms. He's also been in a leadership position at some of the most important organizations in the nation. He is the chairman emeritus of the NAACP Legal Defense and Educational Fund Board of Directors and a fellow of the Harvard Corporation, the governing body of Harvard University. He formerly served as general counsel to the New Jersey NAACP, New Jersey co-chairperson of the United Negro College Fund, and general counsel to the New Jersey Democratic Party—I could go on.

I learned something recently about Ted. Last week we were at a program at the Harvard Law School honoring Professor Charles Ogletree for his service. And I listened as Ted traced the contributions of black lawyers in this country, noting the efforts of Charles Hamilton Houston, Derrick Bell, Charles Ogletree. It was quite a history lesson. He talked about how these amazing lawyers had been a bridge from the civil rights movement to today. Ted Wells is one of those bridges.

Tonight, these four legal stars are going to have an opportunity to talk, and you're going to have the opportunity to eavesdrop on this conversation. I've asked them to be provocative, to express positions that may not be their own but they know exist in the field.

I want to start with a question that seems to permeate conversations about the future of America: Do you see concerns around race as static, and something that will always be with us? Or, do you think that these are concerns that society will eventually overcome?

Ted Wells: I would like to say that at some point, society will overcome issues of race. But I believe that day is beyond the lifetime of anybody in this room, and any children you may have. And perhaps any children they may have. When I was in law school at Harvard, my mentor was Professor Derrick Bell, and he remained my mentor right up until the time he passed away. When Derrick

left Harvard, he came to NYU, so he c⸺ both schools and especially their African⸺ can law students. Derrick had the view⸺ ism ran so deep in this country that th⸺ possibility we would never be able to d⸺

Now, I've not adopted that pessimi⸺ Derrick's, only because if I did, I don't t⸺ get out of bed in the morning. And I⸺ through the day. Derrick was able t⸺ the day because he believed that ev⸺ might not be able to eradicate raci⸺ obligation to confront it. He believ⸺ ous experience to fight a righte⸺ though you might not win it.

I don't think I need to answ⸺ cal question of whether we car⸺ in the next two hundred ye⸺ basic view—and I'm going t⸺ mistic twist—was that we l⸺ historical context. I was b⸺ ington, DC. At that time, decision in 1954—then you don't become so pessimistic. Instead, you recognize that because slavery began in the early 1600s and continued for about two hundred and fifty years, and we then had almost one hundred years of Jim Crow, we're essentially all starting fresh now—whites and blacks. We're kind of early in the game.

I think of America from that perspective when I consider that in my lifetime I've seen an African American president and two African American attorney generals, and I've become the co-chair of litigation at Paul, Weiss, while my law school classmate, Ken Chenault, became the CEO of American Express, another law school classmate, Ken Frazier, became the CEO of Merck, and another law school classmate, Debra Lee, became the CEO of BET. In the same time period, a Paul, Weiss associate whom I mentored, Hakeem Jeffries, became a congressman from Brooklyn, rose to the number five position in the Democratic caucus and is now positioned to do much bigger things.

You can take an optimistic view if you take a historical perspective. My real message to young people is: I know all of you talk about getting "woke," but I want you to understand that we are in a continuing battle for equality. You should learn your history and understand that this is a continuum.

It was somewhat easy for my generation to be in constant fighting mode, because we truly came up in the midst of the civil rights era and the Black Power movement. When we look at John Lewis, we remember his activist days in SNCC— we have a whole different perspective. Our entire lives have been devoted to this battle, and I want to make sure that the next generation understands that we're passing the baton, and that the battle is going to go on for at least another hundred years. So saddle up.

Finally, it's important to recognize that to win this battle, we need a multiracial coalition of whites, blacks, Latinos, and Asians struggling together to achieve equality.

Tony Thompson: Lisa, how do you address this whole issue of the arc of the discussion of race in the country, and how do you see it going?

Lisa Davis: I guess I would say I have a similar perspective, but what's a little different, and what could be scary for younger folks now, is that there has been a retrenchment. There are things going on—things being said, by people in positions of power—that I have not seen in my lifetime. And that's scary. But the only way out is through. We can't hide from it. Our grandparents went through much worse. We have a lot more resources. Folks back then did a lot with a lot less. So whether you're in law firms, or end up in companies, or in Legal Aid, or the Legal Defense Fund—there are more of us, and we have more resources. So we have an obligation.

One of the things that I take seriously is that we take an oath to uphold the Constitution and the laws of the United States. That's number one. Number two: none of us would be here but for Thurgood Marshall, Constance Baker Motley, Robert Carter, Jack Greenberg. Therefore, we owe it to them. I know that Judge Motley's secretary used to go down South with a gun in her purse. Judge Motley didn't have one, but her secretary did. She's felt that . . . "Look, they know who you are, I'm just some black woman with a typewriter in her bag, so I'm going to have a gun." So, I'm just saying it could be worse—scary as all this is, we also have to realize that we have a lot more resources and we're going to have to draw upon them in order to move things forward.

Tony Thompson: Debo, is there a role for law firms to change the national conversation around race? Because it's not happening with the leadership out of Washington at this point.

Debo Adegbile: I think that's an interesting question, because obviously law firms have their own challenges in this space. In order to lead, you have to look inside your organization and think about what you're doing. But we do have special talents as lawyers, we have special abilities. One of the things that's interesting is to think about responses that have come from lawyers in big firms to some of the national policy efforts. Some have come from clients, frankly. Early on, some of the stuff related to the travel ban and the like, some corporations stepped up. And you find yourself in this weird situation, wondering if there is going to be a statement of inclusion that's stronger from corporate America—recognizing some of the exigencies of its global businesses— than there's going to be from electeds who are supposed to be taking an oath to uphold the Constitution and the flag.

I think that law firms can play a role, but

lawyers—and we used to be very mindful of this at the Legal Defense Fund—we were the *lawyers* to the movement. Other people led. So, I think law firms can play a role, but I don't see law firms as being the tip of the spear, as it were. Lawyers are generally conservative, and law firms are generally conservative also, and comprised of many different individuals. I think that there are things that can be done, for sure, but I think it might overstate the case to suggest that the leading edge of change is going to come from law firms.

When I was a student, Derrick Bell gave a great talk about his time and his career. You know that he quite publicly gave up some of his important positions, including as the first tenured African American professor at Harvard Law School, over a principled stance that the University at that time had not tenured an African American woman. He then went on to Oregon and protested there when he encountered similar resistance, and ultimately wound up at NYU, where he ended his illustrious career.

One of the things he said to us was, "People call me a radical. I'm not a radical. I'm a law professor. If I were a radical, I'd be in a tree with a gun. I'm just teaching the law." While I'm not suggesting folks climb trees and arm themselves in response, I am suggesting that sometimes, to have an understanding of where you are in the structure of society, and, to Lisa's point, to think what you can do from the platform you're in, is very important. But I wouldn't want to overstate the case and say that the grand marshal of the parade is going to be big law. My expectation is that that's not going to happen, which doesn't in any way undermine some of the important and significant victories that big law, or the profession in general, can contribute to.

Tony Thompson: Let me turn and talk a little bit more about law firms. We said at the outset that law firms have been slow to appreciate diversity. Damaris, how do you deal with being one of the few, or the first, in your law firm? And what are the challenges that that presents for you?

Damaris Hernández: Well, depending on the day it's a pressure or a privilege. As the first Latina partner at Cravath, I need to make sure I'm not the last. One way I focus on that is by using my platform to make sure that I'm a role model. I want people to see that it is possible to be in a position of power in big law as a person of color.

I also make sure that big law firms, like my own, create a safe space for people to feel that they can come in, they can be supported, they can have opportunities, they can find mentors, and they can get promoted. This is me being not delusional but hopeful. It's my role as a person of color in leadership at my firm to make sure it happens. The pressure is making sure that I speak to kids in college and law school and say, "Look, you too can do it. I'm not special. I just was resilient. I knew what I wanted. I sought the opportunities. I sought mentors. I believed in myself. And others believed in me along the way."

Then, I also go and talk to other people in power in my firm, and make sure that they understand the benefits of diversity and that they are aware of any perceptions impacting the people of color who are deciding *not to come* to our firm and choosing a different path. We need to examine why it is that people self-select out. Do they not think they're supported or wanted in our spaces? Do they not think that they belong there because there's no one like them on the letterhead? Are they like me, who even two years in, walked into that marble building thinking, "Today's the day they're going to find out I'm a fraud"? That self-impostor syndrome doesn't leave just because you have a title. When you're first generation and when you don't see people like you in those halls, you think, "I fell in through the cracks." Nope. I actually walked in that door and showed them that I bring value. That's what everybody has to do, and we have to support our young people and let them know that they have value-add and that they belong in these firms.

Tony Thompson: So how do the rest of you deal with the challenges of being one of the few partners of color in a firm?

Lisa Davis: I am not afraid to speak up, and it's a relatively small firm—we're eighty lawyers. I was fortunate—and I think Damaris touched on this—in terms of having mentors. I had people at the firm who were supportive at the outset. But the other thing—and I think this is key for people of color—is you cannot go into a firm, just put your head down and work, and not develop relationships. That is a mistake I see people make, particularly in big law. They think, "I'm just going to outwork everybody." Well, you're not going to be able to.

Not to say that you're not going to work hard and do excellent work, but the other thing that I did is develop relationships outside of the firm. I was in the community, involved in politics. So for example, one of my partners, when I was an associate, went to a meeting and ran into Gordon Davis. And the partner tells me, "Gordon Davis speaks very highly of you, how do you know Gordon Davis?" And I'm like, "Let me worry about how I know Gordon Davis. All I know is that you went somewhere, you were in negotiation, and a partner at another firm knew about me." And those kinds of relationships are a form of insurance. Because if you're just an anonymous person of color who has no relationships, in some environments they will feel that you can't contribute to the firm in a meaningful way.

And I think it's important to pick your firm. I was teasing Damaris because I was a summer associate at a particular firm, and my joke about my time as a summer associate is that they were so sexist they never noticed I was black. Literally, the first day I went in, I decided I was going to do a rotation in corporate, and they said to me, "A woman? In corporate? A trailblazer!" I was like, "Am I in a DeLorean, and have we gone back several decades? What the heck!" So when I finished my clerkship, I purposefully chose a firm that was known as being a little bit more nimble and liberal (though I was still the only black lawyer in the place). You should pick the environment, recognizing that some environments are more hospitable than others.

Damaris Hernández: I echo that you can't go into a firm and *just* work hard; however, the first two years at any firm are critical. You need to be excellent. Your work product must be stellar. You need to build your brand. You need to show that you're confident, you're trustworthy, reliable, that you're a badass. Build your credibility by delivering excellent work product.

But then, as Lisa said, you also need to build relationships. Most workplaces are in need of more diversity, so you can't expect the one brown partner to be your mentor. You need to find mentors and sponsors and people that don't look like you. And you need to find more than one. I call it having your board of directors. You have one mentor who will help you navigate the policies of the organization. You'll have one who will show you how to have a successful career. You have another director who tells you how to manage having two kids while you're an associate, and then, still become a partner at a firm. While it is always helpful to find people who share your experiences, your background, and commonalities, you also need to identify mentors who are different from you. You actually want people who have been through what lies ahead for you, who know how to navigate the workplace and who are respected enough that if they say, "Hey, she's good," people are going to believe you're good even if they've never worked with you.

Tony Thompson: There are a couple of things you all have said in public consistently. One is that the first order of business is to be excellent at what you do, to be good at your craft. I always tell my students that's the first order of business. But all of you also talk about the power of mentors. How do you identify people you want to mentor you?

Debo Adegbile: So, picking up on Damaris's point, my fundamental contention is that great lawyers are not born, they're made. There is nobody who is born a great lawyer. Thurgood Marshall wasn't born a great lawyer. Charles Hamilton was not born a great lawyer. Justice Sotomayor was not born a great lawyer. Great lawyers are made through experience, through hard work. Through studying the craft, through making mistakes, through taking some lumps and getting back up and learning from them. And from connecting with people who are willing to invest in you, take you under their wing, and help guide you in whatever environment you're in.

I studied a number of courses on race and the law with the late great A. Leon Higginbotham, who was a terrific mentor. He was many things, but he was also a terrific mentor. He had been the chief judge of the Third Circuit Court of Appeals, and after he stepped down from the court, he was affiliated with a firm and he also taught. And A. Leon took a real interest in young lawyers and in lawyers who wanted to go up into the world and be involved in the fight for justice. And so, frankly, I picked my initial post-graduation firm in large part because A. Leon was there. And I wanted to get close to A. Leon, because he was somebody who had manifested an interest in guiding young lawyers and investing his time in that way.

In some ways, the path that I have taken from there to where I sit right now was based on that bet that I placed—that A. Leon was going to take an interest in me. My first voting case as a summer associate was with A. Leon at Paul, Weiss, and then I kept doing that, in large part because of opportunities that came to me from working with A. Leon and others who were in his sphere of influence and had similar inspirations.

Once Ted Wells came to Paul, Weiss, I knew it was okay for me to go, because there was somebody in charge who was going to handle things. So I went to the NAACP Legal Defense Fund to litigate voting cases. That's a straight line from being a student with aspirations but not knowing how to do it, to taking a step out there and following somebody who nurtured not just me but scores of lawyers. He was as proud of his former clerks as he was of any opinion that he drafted or any achievement or plaque on his wall. He would speak about his mentees often, and he really felt that that was his contribution. So the contribution I try to make is to give back in some small way to lawyers who are looking for guidance in their careers. I walked into the building tonight on the phone with a new associate at the firm. It was his first call for guidance, and we were talking something through.

Tony Thompson: So not only are you all trying to develop young lawyers, but you're trying to take care of your own business as well; how do you balance that in making those decisions?

Ted Wells: If you are going to be a person of consequence, then you are going to have to be a player in multiple arenas. Everything starts with hard work.

If you are at a law firm, you need to work hard and be excellent there, because that's what we're selling. We're selling judgment and excellence by the hour. That's how we're able to charge what we charge. People come to us with their problems, and we need to be able to say: "I'm the best person to deal with your problem, but you're going to pay me a lot of money to deal with it." And if you're not a good lawyer, people are not going to pay you what you want to charge.

Then, if you're concerned about helping your community, you're going to have to work hard there. When I started practicing law, I tried to be the hardest working associate in my firm, but I tell people all the time: "Don't focus on only your law firm." When I was a first-year associate, I joined a black bar association, and that became my base, because it put me in contact with other young black lawyers. One of our first challenges was to run the congressional campaign of a young black woman. We had no idea how to run a campaign. But this young black woman said, "I want to run," and we said, "we're down." We learned how to raise money and how to get people registered. Unfortunately, she lost, but this effort laid the foundation for future success.

Our black bar association developed a group that eventually managed the campaign of another black candidate, Donald Payne, who won and served in Congress for twenty-one years. Out of that political work, not only did we learn how to run campaigns, but we also developed a professional network that many of us would tap into for the next thirty to forty years. Because we started young and stuck together, we didn't let our law firms separate us from our community.

As a young lawyer, I also started doing volunteer work for the Legal Defense Fund and the NAACP. Early on in my career, despite all the work I had to do for my law firm, I did not let the firm define my life. What you do in those early years is critical.

You also need mentors. When I started practicing in 1976, you could count the number of black partners in the United States on one hand. In fact, most of us were the only black lawyers in our firms—there were no black partners, and no other black associates. So our mentors were white. I had multiple mentors, including a partner who was a great trial lawyer, as well as several senior associate mentors.

You need mentors who can give you different types of mentorship. When I was writing my first brief, I couldn't go to my partner mentor and ask him to review it before I turned it in, because that brief was for him! I wanted to make sure my brief was excellent, so I asked a senior associate to look at it and tell me if I got it right. The associates will have time to review your work. A senior partner may have the greatest heart in the world, but he's not going to have that much free time. I'll be candid with you: don't ask me to look at your brief—I'm sixty-seven years old. No. You'd better bring it to me correct.

You're going to need community mentors— people who are going to show you the roles you can play there. I tell every black or Latino lawyer I meet: "If you want to participate in your community, and you've been lucky enough to get a law degree, you'll be welcomed with open arms." For example, every Latino and African American politician needs a lawyer. They all have legal issues, and they don't have the money to go to a firm, but you can donate your services to them, all in compliance with campaign finance laws. You want to play? All you have to do is raise your hand. Just know that when you raise your hand, so many people will ask for help that you might have to take a step back.

There are other opportunities to be a player in your community. For example, charter schools all need lawyers to help them. You can serve on nonprofit boards. That's how I learned how to be a board member and how to run a board meeting. But I didn't wait until I was forty or fifty—I started in my twenties.

All of the relationships that you develop as a young person start to bear fruit years later. You will work with people who go on to become leaders, and you will become part of the leadership circle too, because you grew up together.

Debo Adegbile: I think Lisa and Ted have both made a point about the inside/outside game, which is an important theme of success in legal careers. It's been important, I think, to all of us. But I daresay it's going to be more important for the young lawyers in this room, because the law is changing, and economies are changing so quickly that you're probably likely to have even more legal jobs than we've had in our lives. And what you're trying to do is build a set of skills, a reputation, and a network that is going to sustain you and help you pivot through these different experiences.

There's an inherent tension in what we're talking about, because Damaris came in on the first point, which is, it doesn't matter how many people you know, if you're not bringing the brief correct to Ted, or your loan documents are a mess—that's not going to solve it for you. You have to come correct.

You have to be prepared with the technical law-yering skills, and that takes upfront investment. It takes investment throughout, but it takes more investment upfront. There's no way around that.

But as you go through your career, you have to be thinking about: What are the things that matter to you, and how do you carve out that time to be connected to them? Ted mentioned many different ones: politics, not-for-profits, other organizations. Maybe it's your religious affiliation in your church or synagogue. Whatever it is, think about those different connections, because the law, more than almost any other profession, is about the network and who you're connected to.

That is true whether you're going for a government job, and the FBI is going to your elementary school to check in on you—which happens, I'm here to tell you—or you're somebody like myself, who had been in big law, then in a not-for-profit for a long time, then in government, and then, through some unexpected circumstances, back in big law sooner than I had expected to be. Having people who will vouch for you, who know you, those with whom you've made a contribution in different contexts—that is what enables each of those situations. The value assigned to that type of network, while you're carrying your toolbox with you, is really something of tremendous importance for all lawyers, but especially for lawyers of color.

Tony Thompson: I'm going to pick up on that point, because it's exactly what I wanted to ask. Some of the things you're talking about have to do with lawyering and being competent. But is there a unique role for partners of color, both internally for the firm, and externally for the country? And if there is a unique role, how do you manage that?

Lisa Davis: Well, I think it's not unique to law partners of color. Academics of color talk about the double burden that they have to bear too. We are ambassadors, and we get trotted out in certain circumstances. We are, by default, the mentors for all the associates of color. So those things happen. You're an ambassador both externally and internally. I think a lot of us end up being the conscience of the law firm.

I do think that part of what you have to do is be comfortable enough in your own skin and know which microaggression—among many—you're going to ignore. That's why having a network outside of the office is important. You go home and say to your significant other, or your buddies, "You know what so-and-so said to me today . . . ?" Because you're not going to lose it in the office.

Damaris Hernández: You could do it if you close the door. I'm just saying, now, you spend a lot of hours in that place.

Lisa Davis: I'm in a small law firm with thin walls . . . in any case, I think that's part of what you have to do.

Damaris Hernández: I want to pivot on something Lisa just said: "You have to feel comfortable in your skin." We've been talking about doing very good work, and building relationships. The third thing you need to focus on is being true to yourself. You may have a feeling that you need to check your identity at the door when you get to big law. This is not true. If you aren't comfortable in your own skin, you're going to burn out because our jobs are too demanding to have to fake the funk while you're working 24/7.

You need to embrace the fact that your experiences and your background are advantages, and you need to use that perspective to benefit yourself, and make the firm appreciate that it's a benefit for them. I made partner, and the whole time I was unapologetically Latina. I was open about my experiences growing up because that's what makes me who I am. My hard work—one of the values that firms appreciate—was because my mama told me, "You got to work twice as hard to get half as much." That work ethic that they embraced and they loved—and that got me promoted—existed because of who I am, and I just needed to be comfortable enough in my own skin to take pride in that.

Debo Adegbile: I think that most of us do have special roles to play in our firms. It's hard to avoid. In fact, you'd have to affirmatively reject the role. You'd have to make an affirmative statement, maybe not out loud, to not engage in this work and not recognize that there aren't as many folks who look like you, or not as many who have had your experiences. Some people make that choice and put their head down. There are people who close the door to their office, and just kill it and bill time.

Part of it is defining "being comfortable in your skin," and also, what is the commitment you've made to be a professional. What does it mean to occupy space as a rare lawyer of color in a profession where there aren't enough? And does the job, the name on the door, affect what your self-definition is? Sometimes there are trade-offs in big firms, because there are hours targets and you have to bring in new business if you're a partner—there are many things that are going to be pulling on you. And one could decide, *I don't have time for this committee. I don't have time to sit down with this person, because it's coming out of my time at the end of the day.*

But when you have come through this process, when people have made time for you, when you understand the history that brought you to have the opportunity, for me, it's easy to make that time. The other pressure is on your family. Because some of that time and your generosity of spirit or commitment to mentor others . . . there are only so many hours in the day. Every board you're on, every call you take, every piece of advice you give, every diversity committee meeting, every follow-up call to a recruit—it's coming out of somebody's time.

Balancing these competing interests is a challenge of the double/triple/quadruple-however-many-burdens-you-want-to-talk-about. I think a lot of it is deciding how you want to walk through the world, and, at the end of the day, how you are going to measure success. I measure success not only by trying to kill it for my clients, but also by trying to make a way for others. Because without people willing to try to do that for me, there is no possibility I would have had the opportunities I've had.

Tony Thompson: We're in an ecosystem where I don't see enough students of color, or enough faculty of color, at the law school. And each type of institution has different things we try to do. What are the types of things that firms can do to increase diversity? How do we think about that? I think about it when I think about faculty going back to law students and affecting their experience. What are the types of things that firms can do?

Ted Wells: The biggest thing firms can do is offer minority law students jobs, and hope that many of them accept. It's no different than when a college accepts a certain number of students, and tries to get the best yield. Now, that's looking at the issue from the very narrow perspective of a particular firm. The reality is, Paul, Weiss is competing for the same small group of minority students as Cravath and WilmerHale.

I want the students who come to my firm to love it. But I'm at the point in my life now when I look at things holistically instead of thinking from the perspective of only Paul, Weiss or only the New York City legal community. Every firm's got a personality. If I thought a particular black, Latino, or Asian student was a better fit for another firm, I'd direct them to that place. I tell law students that if they want to work at a big firm, I want to make sure they're going to a firm that not only has a reputation for excellence, but also has an environment where I think they are going to be mentored, and they are going to be given a chance to succeed.

My biggest recruiting pitch to any minority student—and I say this with great sincerity—is if you've got a problem, you can come to my office, and I can try to deal with it. I have the potential to be the enforcer if I think something is not going down correctly.

Some firms have a better sensitivity to diversity issues than others. When you're interviewing, you have to look at that firm's history and ask, "How many minority partners are there? Are the minority partners at that firm in positions of influence, where they will be listened to? Where they can be the conscience of the firm?" Because you can't serve as the conscience of the firm if people don't want to listen to you. At some firms, when you raise issues of social justice, other lawyers might ignore you, or only pretend to listen to you. Speaking loudly can help, but you need to be at a firm where you will be respected. Because all firms don't have the same level of respect or sensitivity for diversity, you've got to do your research.

Lisa Davis: People probably know about the study that the diversity consultant Arin Reeves did of law firm partners. She created two identical copies of a legal memo, with intentional mistakes in it. One copy said it was written by "Bill Merryweather III, NYU Law grad." The other said something like "Marcus Johnson, NYU Law grad"—in other words, everything was the same except the ethnicity. With the memo from the white associate, people overlooked some of the mistakes. They said, "Oh, he just needs a little coaching, he seems like he has promise." On the black memo, they caught every mistake and said, "I don't even understand how he got in to NYU." That's concrete evidence of real, implicit racism. I'm not going to call it bias—that's racism. So one thing that you could do, in terms of pipeline and résumés, is to blank out anything that identifies

60

the race of the applicant. And then see what kind of yield you get.

Another thing you could do is to hire laterals. At my firm, we really don't hire people right out of school. But firms can devise mechanisms—I hate to say "tests," because people who come out of law school don't want to take any more tests— but if you're hiring a lateral and it's a corporate person, you can say, "Alrighty, draft this agreement for me." You may not want to give someone a research assignment, but, on the transactional side, if you're hiring someone with some experience, you can say, "Mark this up and let's see what the comments look like," and do it blind. Those are some things, if you really want to get nitty-gritty, that you can do.

Damaris Hernández: I think firms need to attack this on three fronts: recruitment, retention, and promotion. On recruitment, you need to expand the criteria that we use to actually get people in the door. Law firms focus on school tiers, school grades, and law review, and those should not be the only criteria we're looking at. When I'm interviewing people, I look to see whether they have the grit and determination to be successful. I look at them from a holistic vantage point. Is this someone who had to care for their sick mother or work twenty hours to support their family while they were in law school, and their grades aren't stellar because of that? Or they decided to go to a lower-tier school because they were getting a full ride? That's the type of analysis we need to do at the recruitment level. We need to look beyond top schools, grades, and law review.

Then, once you actually get the people in the building, you need to make sure that they're getting meaningful work, support, mentorship, sponsorship, and professional development. You need to create safe spaces, so they feel like they can be heard. Then, we need to promote people! If you can't see it, you can't achieve it. If you don't see people like you on that letterhead, you either think you don't belong there, or they don't want you there—which might not be true.

This goes back to the question of, "What is our unique role as partners of color?" We not only need to be role models and use our platform to get together with like-minded people and leverage our collective strengths. We need to go a step further. We also need to speak to our non-brown counterparts and explain to them why they need to be invested in diversity efforts and why they need to champion attorneys of color. We need to move beyond this notion of "colorblindness." A lot of times they don't want to have the dialogue because they don't want to be misunderstood and mislabeled. My view is, "Have the dialogue with me because I have thick skin and I can set you straight." That's one of my roles—to engage others in uncomfortable conversations.

Lisa Davis: I want to push back a little bit on what

you said, not because I disagree, but because I don't know how realistic it is. I feel that black and Latino lawyers suffer from what I call the "affirmative action discount." Whatever school we go to, they assume we got in through "affirmative action," which in their view means lower standards. And we confront that implicit bias. If you say, "Well, for students of color, let's go to a different tier school and not pay attention to grades," aren't you potentially compounding what those students are going to confront? I'm not saying you shouldn't do it. Even one of my white colleagues agrees that we have to do this, or we're not going to get more people of color. And I think you're right. But how do you deal with the bias these young lawyers of color are going to confront?

Damaris Hernández: To clarify, I look for people— from all backgrounds–who have grit, hunger, and ownership. Those are the people who are successful in law. This isn't an approach limited to people of color. That said, I believe that most first-generation immigrants and most people of color had to have grit, resilience, and a strong work ethic to get to the place where they are either applying to law school or law firms.

Now that I'm on this side, I have a say in recruiting. When I see a résumé that's borderline, I say, "It isn't going to cost us anything to invite somebody into the office and interview them." Ultimately, it might be a no, but you might be surprised when they sit in front of you and they can occupy that professional space despite what their résumé says, and they can handle their own.

I can share my experience: I was not top of my class at NYU, but I am a hell of an interviewee and I worked my ass off to get here. I made sure that whoever was on the other side of my interview understood that. Yes, it may be a challenge to convince the organization, but the only way that we're actually going to make any change is if we push back on expectations, the same way you pushed back on me. I'll win some of these, I'll lose some, but at some point there'll be somewhere that gives.

I think there are additional ways to address the issue of being viewed as pounding on the table for another person of color just because they are a person of color or because you're trying to "raise your numbers." One of the ways to deal with that is similar to the way you ask students to make sure they are building relationships. I do the same thing. I may not pound the table, but I'll work behind the scenes to make sure people who do pound the table know that a particular person is stellar. I make sure that the people who are at that table are aware of the people coming up who are valuable, who are an asset, who need to be at our firm, and who might not be known by everybody. I make sure that I advocate for them.

Ted Wells: The law students the large firms prize the most are the ones who were on law review. That's their litmus test. I say all the time: "I wasn't on the Harvard Law Review." Of course, many law students who were *magna cum laude* become outstanding associates. But others with excellent grades do not thrive in law firms or have the right skill set for private practice. So I reject the narrow focus on law review.

I also reject the narrow focus on straight A's. So what if you have a B? I think that's all nonsense. I don't think there's an empirically proven correlation between being a great lawyer and being able to ace a two-hour law school exam.

It's no different than the forty-yard dash in the NFL. A fast time in the forty-yard dash doesn't mean that you're a good football player, it just means you succeeded in the test they use to measure you. Law firms are paying associates $150,000 to $180,000 a year. Based on only a few twenty-minute interviews, they have to make hiring decisions. When deciding whether to pay a law student nearly $200,000, the best information the firms have to rely on is a transcript. So that's what they use.

If big law firms stick to the narrow criteria of law review credentials and straight A's, it's unlikely that they will have many black associates, because there is not enough supply of black or Latino students who meet those criteria to satisfy the hiring demands of the major law firms. So I believe we should have more flexibility in the hiring criteria, because many law students who have the ability to be great lawyers—black, white, or from other ethnic groups—do not fit the law-review/straight-A model.

Ultimately, we should relax the traditional criteria and take some chances to expand the pool of minority associates. Sometimes we'll hit home runs, sometimes we'll strike out. But the same thing happens with the law review people! Some are great, and some are not so great.

Lisa asked, "Does that increase the possibility of people having affirmative action bias?" I don't care if it increases bias. In fact, the bias may be there anyway. My view is that large law firms should hire as many qualified minority associates as possible and give them a fair opportunity to succeed.

I believe if enough minority students come in the door, some will become top-tier lawyers, and even those who are not stellar will benefit. They will have a big firm name on their résumés, get exposure to mentors, and learn how to practice law—and most of them will go on to have great careers. In my view, academic credentials do not determine your destiny as a lawyer. If you have grit, determination, and gumption, you're going to do fine.

Tony Thompson: Are there things that law schools can be doing that will help students succeed at firms?

Debo Adegbile: I think that's an interesting question,

and I know there are conversations going on throughout the legal academy about how to train lawyers. One of the things that I guess we've touched upon in different ways is that there are different skills that you need to succeed in a law firm, and law firms need people with different skills too. That's not to say that you can get to a law firm and not have some level of core technical skills within your discipline. But I take Ted's point, that we have some folks who may be great at writing the brief and great at marking up the transactional documents, but Lord, would you ever put them with a client? It just wouldn't happen. And they're not likely to bring in the business, which is the lifeblood of the firms that are prepared to pay for Ted and Lisa's talents.

I think that law schools have to be in the conversation. You have to be thinking about what the profession requires in the future. And I think some of the other skills—some of the things that Damaris was talking about—are coming to be understood by people who are studying the science of the skills that are the indicia of success. Some studies are being done in that regard, and that's something that law schools need to look at on the way in the door, because law schools have their own version of the law review that they apply on the threshold level. And if everybody just keeps chasing the same narrow group of folks, then you don't expand the pool.

To be sure, we need to do pipeline stuff that expands the pool and has more people that perhaps can hit those traditional markers. But it's really silly not to look broadly for the folks who have the talent and the capability. I think law schools can think about their criteria and their curriculum. They can lead in a sense by showing success. Different quantums of success that firms can be open to.

I also want to add one point to the previous conversation, because it was implicit but not explicit: leadership matters a lot in diversity. It's important to have firm leaders who are holding their firms to account for improving things. When I was at NYU Law there was a City Bar initiative to make diversity better at law firms—I know I look like I'm fifteen, but I'm fifty—and the conversation is much the same today. To be sure, we've made some progress, but you can just pull up the articles—go back and look at the *American Lawyer*, and they're the same articles about the same difficulties.

So it's critical to have some firms and firm leaders who are making an affirmative commitment to move the dial—to change things and to go boldly in that direction, perhaps to show what it looks like to lead, and then folks will follow. It happens with salaries, it's going to happen with diversity. The American Bar Association has a resolution out now, and clients are very focused now on diversity, and are beginning to measure firms, in part, in terms of diversity, including with some incentives in some cases. There are a set of dynamics in the world right now that create possibilities, so that the *American Lawyer* articles in fifteen or twenty more years are not going to be the same as they have been for the last twenty years.

Tony Thompson: How else do we convert firm leadership to take this on as a leadership issue within the firm—to say, "Diversity means something to us"? Obviously, finance will drive a lot of that conversation, but what are the other things that drive that conversation?

Debo Adegbile: I think part of it has to do with the leaders, the people you choose to lead. And that's gender, that's race; it's experience. There are a whole range of different things. I think today there was an article that a firm picked an African American leader as the managing partner—somebody flipped it to me while I was in a meeting today. It has to do in part with whom you're vesting with the responsibility to lead you. Because there are folks who will keep doing things in the way that they've done them.

I was on the recruiting committee at Paul, Weiss; I'm on the recruiting committee at WilmerHale. There will always be a certain number of folks who are looking to recreate the world in their image. It's the same problem with federal clerkships. It's a problem across our profession. But then there are going to be those who are pushing the envelope in the ways that Damaris and Ted and Lisa at their own firms are, who are thinking about, "What are the indicia of success?" And, "Let me tell you about what my experiences have been that fit both profiles—both the ones that fit your perfect measure and came in and couldn't get it done, and were out in a year, and folks that perhaps were the little engine that could, and are killing it."

I have gone to bat for associates who may not have been bright and shiny when they came in, but these are people who practice leaders go to all the time—I'm now worried I brought these people to the firm and they have too much work! But that's the type of thing you have to do, you have to go to bat. You have to say, "Don't make this mistake. This person has a demonstrated track record of success." We don't need everybody to have the same charisma. Sometimes it matters that you can do the work and do it well.

Tony Thompson: Damaris, you're probably the closest to the end of the pipeline on this panel. What have you seen that's worked in terms of pipeline issues? What are the things that we need to replicate?

Damaris Hernández: We need to be visible. That's the first step. When I became partner I received a lot of notes in the mail from students who were in law school, students who were pre-law, students who were in high school and they had seen the *New York Times* article, and they were like, "Holy crap. I am from Brooklyn. Holy crap, I'm Latina. Wow.

You're an example." Part of the solution is letting people see that they can achieve it. They need to see someone like them, from their background.

Then, again, it goes back to making sure that we're looking beyond numbers and that we have committed leaders. We can't just wait for people to move on. We need to be the examples. I push back a lot because I am invested in recruiting. I recruit a lot. I was the first Latina partner, I don't plan to be the last. I don't have patience, so I can't sit there by myself for too long. I get lonely. I make sure that I go back and I say, "Look, I sold this place to ten people who are coming this year and you are not going to make me look bad because my word is my word. You can't mess up my street cred, so you need to make sure that I can deliver on what I said this place is willing to do in terms of its diversity and inclusion efforts. And I'm not doing it by myself. Some of you have to join me."

Once you get in the ear of some, at some point those some are going to grow. And some other people are going to fall off. You can create change. It'll take a while—I can't guarantee when it's going to happen . . . I hope it happens in my lifetime. Tony, you scared me when you opened this conversation! I have a two-year-old and a six-year-old and I hope it happens in their lifetime. People call it a burden. I see it as a privilege. Sitting in Brooklyn on my steps, I never thought I'd be sitting here with Ted Wells!

Tony Thompson: We've talked about mentorship. I appreciate Debo and Damaris's conversation about leadership at the firm level. Are there strategies you think we should be talking to students of color about, that they should employ to be successful in law firm culture?

Lisa Davis: It's a balance that you have to maintain: you have to stay true to your authentic self. But I tell people, find the thing you have in common with the people that you work with—there's always going to be something. You would be surprised. Everybody loves Drake now, so that's corny—my kids tell me that's corny. But whatever the thing is, find it. For example—because I am corny—I like old Broadway show tunes. One of my mentors is our most senior partner, and if he comes into my office and talks about Hoagy Carmichael, I'm like, "Yeah, 'Stardust,' that's a great song!" It shows that we are connected despite our age, gender, and racial difference. So it's finding that thing—film, TV, *This Is Us*—whatever the thing is, find it.

It's not fair, but the likelihood is that we have much more experience interacting with white people than they have interacting with us. And so part of the burden is to make them comfortable. And that does not mean not being untrue to yourself. I will never forget the time Public Enemy first came to my office, and Flavor Flav showed up two hours late, and the receptionist said, "Lisa, there's a Mister Flav here to see you."

Tony Thompson: "And he doesn't know what time it is . . ."

Lisa Davis: And I'm like, "Brother, you're two hours late and you wear a clock. How does that happen?" But the thing is, I brought Public Enemy in. But at the same time, I'm going to talk about Hoagy Carmichael, or *Man of La Mancha*, or whatever the thing is. And if you scratch the surface with most people, you will find that thing. I happen to be Catholic, so with the Catholic guys, I was like, "Yeah, when you're Catholic like us." Whatever it is! If it's legal and it's not pornographic, I will talk about it.

Ted Wells: I strongly agree with Lisa's point about social relationships, but at the end of the day I think it's more about the work. I tell young associates that your real client is the senior associate for whom you are writing a research memo. That is your client. Or it's the junior partner for whom you're writing the first draft of a brief. At my level, I want to know who will produce written work that I do not have to spend too much time editing. Because if I have to do a rewrite—and there's a difference between editing and a rewrite—then I can't see the Yankees. Or the Giants. No one wants to spend a weekend rewriting poor work product instead of watching the game.

People figure out real quick which associates will make their lives easier. And though social connections are good, work product is better. That's why I say, find a mid-level associate to mentor you, someone who can look at a draft memo or brief before you give it to the person who's going to grade it. Once you get your sea legs, you don't have to keep asking for a preliminary review. Just don't take the chance that you got it right the first time, or that a partner will take the time to teach you if you got it wrong. Let somebody junior teach you offline before you turn in your work product.

I say this because, unfortunately, early impressions can be lasting ones. One of my former partners said: "The man who becomes known as an early riser can sleep till noon." If people get the impression that you turn out first-rate work product, that presumption stays with you. But if you become known as an associate who produces research memos that can't be trusted, and you make the partners look up the cases themselves, pretty soon, they won't want to nurture you. They're going to find someone who can write the research memo well the first time.

People are busy, and they have selfish goals: *Who can make my life easier? Who can make me look good?* You want to make a partner think: "This associate gave me a great brief, and when I give it to the client, I will be viewed as the person with the right team and the right talent." Especially in your early years, first impressions can be last impressions. Don't get off on a bad foot.

Lisa Davis: Ted made it sound as if I was saying that work is not important, and the work *is* important, that goes without saying. But I will say one thing as a follow-up to that—and this is critical for associates of color and women of color in particular: you do not get honest feedback. People are loathe to give you feedback. So all those things Ted is saying are absolutely true. But the other thing I would say is, after every assignment, ask for feedback. Don't wait until the annual review. Say, "How could I have done this better?"

That way, if you did stumble and you're not quite sure . . . a partner of mine calls it eating the death cookie. Basically, it's better to get the bad news early, because, number one, they'll see you want to improve, and two, you will overcome their reticence because they think that women are gonna cry. I don't know if they think brothers are gonna punch them. I don't know what the deal is. But the point is, ask for feedback. Because that's your opportunity.

Another friend of mine said, "Nobody cares about your career as much as you do." The responsibility for your career rests primarily with you. These places are intimidating. Big firm, small firm—doesn't matter. You're working for people who are intimidating. But you have to get over that. Because successful lawyers have confidence. They project confidence to clients. And you may hear things you don't like! One of the things I always say is that the gift of my career was that the first boss I had was a black woman. There was nowhere to hide. When I screwed something up, I knew I had screwed it up. I couldn't hide behind racism, sexism, anything. And it was a great lesson. So that's the other piece of advice I would give.

Tony Thompson: Let me run one last question through all of you. I'm not as quick as Ted or Debo to tell my age, but I've been here a long time, and practiced for a while before that, and we're hearing some things we haven't heard in a long time

coming from the nation's capital and other corners of the country. Reflecting on the twenty-first
century, what advice or message would you want
law students and young lawyers to hear from you
going forward?

Debo Adegbile: There are three things that I think
lead to success in the law. First, it's the toolbox:
developing the core lawyering skills you'll need
in your field. Because the toolbox goes with you.
It's portable. So you don't have to be limited by
any particular situation. You bring those skills
with you. They will open the door to the next
opportunity.

Next—and we've talked a lot about this—is the
relationships. No profession requires this more
than ours does. But what does focusing on relationships mean? It means being a good colleague.
It means reading somebody else's memo. It means
giving a heads-up to somebody about a particular
partner to work with or not to work with. Or how

to succeed in working with that partner, or how they like materials prepared.

A partnership is like a feudal system where each lord likes things in a different way. So you need to learn these things when you come in. And who's going to tell you? Ted's point: you're not going to go to the partner. There's going to be an associate, or a mid-level lawyer who's going to teach you how to navigate in that space.

And all of this goes toward the third thing: your reputation. At the end of the day, what are people going to say about you? What kind of lawyer are you, what kind of person are you? Are you a person of integrity? Your reputation matters. If you tend to those three things—your toolbox, your relationships, and your reputation—you'll have a successful career.

In addition, even when you get into a place like one of our firms, there is a narrow pathway to become partner at any firm. The reason it's so important to be working on these three things is that you don't know what the pathway is going to be for you exactly. That doesn't mean you don't come to a place and try to become Ted Wells. You should. But even Ted Wells became partner at Paul, Weiss by becoming Ted Wells someplace else first. I'm at WilmerHale, and I did other things first. Lisa had different experiences. (Damaris is a different situation. We all want to be like her, where you just get in there and kill it.) But the point here is, really think about those three things, because they will continue with you throughout your career in a range of contexts. You should be open to the things that you want to do now, but also to the things you can't yet see. And if you tend to these three things, you'll be well on your way.

Damaris Hernández: I echo that. I go back to being true to yourself. Remember what your core values are. Remember what you want. You're going to kill it at work. You're going to be successful. But also remember what your priorities are. If you care about family, community, church, hobbies, if you go to the gym, keep doing those things! We need you in big law. You can do good and still make a lot of money, and give back.

I was asked recently during the recruiting season, by an applicant, "Do you feel like a sellout?" I literally gave her a call back just because she had the balls to ask me that. I started by saying, "You had twenty minutes with me and you felt like you could ask that? Girl, I got you." I told her that when I interviewed at Cravath ten years ago, I had the chairman of the firm look at my résumé and say, "It looks like you want to do pro bono. Why are you here?" I said, "Because I need to feed my family. But also because you boast that you're the best at training. And someday I may not be here, but I want to know what I'm up against."

Those were not the right answers, and he must have been tired or something because I received an offer. But I have stayed there for ten years, and I give back. I do pro bono. I'm on the pro bono committee. I have a Title VII case—I go to Alabama once a month, where we're suing Jefferson County, the sheriff's department, and the police for race and sex discrimination in hiring. I oversee the associates who are doing DACA applications, asylum applications, and travel ban work. We wrote an amicus arguing that Title IX prohibits discrimination against transgender individuals, which is before the Supreme Court. We do good work and there is much good work to be done. I sit on boards. My firm donates money to many charitable organizations and causes. Many of these are actions that I couldn't have done had I not been at Cravath. I use the resources of the firm and my own individual resources—that toolbox Debo mentioned—and I give back. When you're considering whether to go to big law or, given the recent events in America, whether you should work in the public interest sector, know that you can use your skills to fight back through big law.

Follow Debo's advice so you can actually be great, and then, follow my advice so that we can address Tony's first question which was, "Can law actually change things?" Yes, the law provides us with a vehicle to challenge a number of injustices. As lawyers, we have a special skillset. As people of color, we offer a different perspective and a different understanding. We are impacted directly by many of the changes taking place, so we have to be the ones that are at the forefront of change. We should not be banking on big law to do it all, but we can try to push them.

Lisa Davis: So I'm not at big law. We have ninety-two lawyers. And I work in culture and the arts. I think there are lots of places where we can be useful as lawyers, whether it's big law and using those resources, or at a firm like ours. We did an amicus brief on the travel ban case for the

Anti-Defamation League, even though we're not a firm of three hundred lawyers. I have partners who are out at protests constantly. I have a partner who started a group, Torah Trumps Hate, and led a group of Orthodox Jewish people at the March for Racial Justice. You don't know how you can make a difference. You don't necessarily have to be in the public sector to make a difference.

The point is—and I do take this seriously—we took an oath to uphold the Constitution. And there are people in Washington trashing the Constitution on a daily basis. To me, all lawyers right now—I don't care what color we are—have to stand up for the rule of law, and we have to stand up for the Constitution. That's a duty that every one of us who graduated from law school has right now. What did Ben Franklin say? "A republic, if you can keep it." And we're only going to keep it if those of us in the profession work to let people know what's in the Constitution. That's what we can do no matter where we are practicing.

Ted Wells: I'll end where I began: know your history. Have an appreciation for the impact of race in the United States, for the role that the legal system has played, and for the change that lawyers can promote. My mother worked in a post office, so I knew once I got out of law school, whatever job I did, I would be far ahead of where my mother had been. And I was willing to take chances. You can't let going to an elite law school paralyze you by making you feel that you have no choice but to work in a big firm and keep your mouth shut. Be true to yourself and don't be afraid to take risks. You may already know that you want to go to a particular firm or become a public interest lawyer. But whatever you do, strive to be the best that you can.

I tell law students all the time: if you waste the opportunity to excel in law school, and you go to your first job having barely gotten the position because you did not work to your full potential in school, and you're happy just to be there, then you are not going to be able to speak truth to power in that workplace. You're going to be so afraid that you will be holding on to the job by your fingernails, and not heard or respected, or willing to speak up.

As Damaris's mother used to say: "We have to be twice as good to go half as far." I was raised on that principle. It may sound fundamentally unfair: "Why should I, because I'm a person of color, have to be twice as good to go half as far?" I accept that it's unfair, but that's still the reality we face in America. It's a continuing struggle, and as long as you understand that and don't assume we are living in a real meritocracy, I think you're going to be okay.

Advice from the Experts

A Roundtable Discussion with Diversity Professionals

The conversation with the partners led to another conversation with key diversity professionals from four top law firms, who added context and specific recommendations for the actions that law firms and law schools might take to address the profound lack of diversity in our profession.

Participants in this conversation included Maja Hazell, global head of diversity and inclusion at White & Case; Kiisha Morrow, head of diversity at Cravath, Swaine & Moore; Danyale A. Price, chief inclusion officer at Paul, Weiss, Rifkind, Wharton & Garrison; and Rachel V. Simmonds-Watson, diversity manager at Debevoise & Plimpton. Their responses have been consolidated and edited; where disagreement existed, different perspectives are noted.

Why are there so few associates and partners of color in law firms?

For one thing, the profession is based on relationships, and relationships across difference are very hard to establish. Relationships are key, starting with getting a campus interview, right through the hiring process, and on to being mentored, getting the right work opportunities, getting the advice you need to do a great job and the feedback you need to improve, and being promoted to more senior positions. And relationships are harder to build with people who are different from you.

The law also isn't a profession that's marketed well to young students. There's been a lot of emphasis on STEM—be a doctor, go into technology, math, science. STEM has really been pushed in our communities. Legal careers haven't received the same sort of attention. Many young people of color learn what their possibilities are from the media. So law isn't a profession that a lot of people of color are often aspiring to. Their only interaction with the legal field is through law enforcement. Law just isn't advertised as the place to go.

And lawyers, almost by definition, are risk-averse. So the status quo remains the status quo. There's little incentive to change; the fact that these firms have historically been made up of white males pretty much predicts the future. Diversity and inclusion are all about change, and these places weren't diverse before.

Lawyers are also trained to look at everything from every different angle, pick everything apart, and embrace skepticism. So that adds another wrinkle. You're looking at a risk-averse population in these structures that have been built around a group of skeptical professionals.

So when a partner goes to a law school to recruit, and a white man and a black woman are sitting in front of him, the notion of picking the black woman brings with it a sense of risk?

Even if it's not top of mind, if you keep doing the same thing, you're going to get the same results. So here you are, a white male partner recruiting; it's just human nature—or the way we're socialized from very, very early on—to be drawn to people who are like ourselves, or people who remind us of ourselves. How many white men are seeing that black woman and saying, "Oh, she reminds me of myself"? Conversely, the black woman candidate is not seeing a white man who reminds her of herself either. So if you just let things play out "naturally," the same results are going to occur. You need to be intentional to reach that black woman or reach that other person who is different from the status quo.

How about from the point of view of young lawyers of color? Why aren't they choosing big law, or, if they do choose it initially, why aren't they sticking with it over the long run?

Many associates go into the legal profession because they have a sense of altruism and they really want to make a difference, so they look to government service or the not-for-profit sphere. They don't see law firms as the place to do it. So you have to convince them that the law firm environment does provide that avenue. There's also a generational issue, where young people don't look forward to the drudgery that they see a lot of law firm practice entailing.

So far, they've just followed the script: college, maybe they've worked for a couple of years, then law school and on-campus interviewing. It's all very easy. Two hundred and fifty different law firms are coming to campus to interview. "All I have to do is get on the list. I'm good." They think it's just a continuation of that approach. So law students come to a firm with that mind-set. And they don't understand that they need to come to law firms with an understanding of how they are going to develop skills and engage in professional development and what to get out of the law firm experience.

To be fair, law firms also do a bait and switch. You come for the summer program, and they are wining you, and they are dining you, and they're taking you to meet this interesting person and sit in on this meeting. Then twelve to thirteen months later, you show up on day one as an associate, and it's, "Here's your shovel, here's your hard hat, here's your lunch pail, go to work." And many young people of color feel like, "I didn't sign up for this."

There's also the problem of the selection process and bias. If you look at the representation of students of color at law firms, both African American and Latino students are underrepresented in summer associate classes in comparison to their representation in law school and the general population. So you already have a smaller pool. Then implicit bias comes into play for African American and Latino students, where recruiting attorneys may ask themselves, "What's been my experience with students who've come through previously?" lumping all recruits of color together and asking, "Is this person going to be like that associate who failed?" There's a sense of taking a higher risk on this person or that person, and that's where the numbers get skewed.

This narrowing of the pool then gets reinforced by African American and Latino students opting out to look for something safer, because they don't have a lot of models of success in the law firm environment, and, generationally, the work is just not attractive.

Even for those associates of color who do decide to work at law firms, their attrition—the dwindling of numbers—is almost immediate. Young associates of color are looking to get out of law firms by the end of year two, typically. And there's a real concern on the part of partners that these associates are not staying long enough to build the relationships or make the connections they will need to have successful careers. So even if you want to leave, what are you going to do next? A lot of young attorneys of color are just churning through after two years, not having reaped everything they could have from the law firm experience, and the firms can barely keep them.

A significant portion of the black, Latino, and Asian graduates from top law schools do decide to start their careers at law firms. But then it's a leaky pipeline. Should firms want to keep these

young attorneys from leaving in two years, what would make the associates want to stay?

First of all, there's the business case. Why should law firms care about the number of partners of color? Why should that even matter? For one thing, at this point, clients demand it. So many of the people who've left the law firms and who've gone in-house, because they saw it as more meritocratic, and more of a chance for success, are now looking to see if there's diversity at the law firms they engage in order to get help. They're demanding it, and they're not seeing it.

Even worse, the clients themselves may have had a bad personal experience at Law Firm X and now have the mentality, "I'll never give you a piece of business ever again. You didn't treat me well, so why would I trust that you've done better since then?" Partners are really starting to see that now, especially with women, as more of them ascend to general counsel positions. At this point 25 to 40 percent of new general counsels are women.

If we then look at the lead time to partnership, the pipeline is not just leaky, it has really fundamental holes in it. About 1 percent of the partners at New York law firms are African American. And that may be generous. Are there unique challenges that lawyers of color face as they try to climb into partnership ranks?

It's tough to become a partner. You have to develop relationships, you have to have the right exposure, you have to have the right sponsorship. And just for starters, it can be lonely. If you are one of the few partners of color at your firm, or even looking across firms, if we assume that there is a distinct experience that you are having, finding no one to go through that experience with you is isolating. Seeing people leave law firms, and seeing the turnover at the partner level is also disheartening—it's not just confined to white men; partners of color are leaving their law firms to go to other law firms, or just leaving the whole system. And some of that is clearly because, "I'm the only person." So it's a lonely existence at times.

Most senior attorneys of color have an added tax in a law firm: their role is not only to produce whatever the legal product is, but also to pave a way for other folks of color, making sure that they succeed. That's their added responsibility. We see individual instances of senior people taking a specific associate of color under their wing; how do we make that happen more broadly, outside that one individualized experience?

Everyone at the table needs to do that. And that's also why firms have diversity professionals. People literally ask us, "Well, what do you do? What is your day-to-day?" And at some level, our job, day-to-day, is making people in a high-pressured, high-stress environment slow down enough to invest in someone who is different from them.

The associates of color are looking at the partners of color to be their mentors, and it's good for the partners to feel connected to the associates of color. But at the same time, the partners need to be focused on what's going to help them excel and get into positions of leadership. Partners of color are stretched in so many ways: your firm wants you to be on the recruiting side, they want you to be on every brochure, and you still need to be building your book of business.

So there are a number of different things pulling on partners of color. And they may also have other ambitions: a lot of them want to become general counsels at a company, or take on additional levels of responsibility at their current firms or enter public service. So it's the tax of being everybody's mentor, everybody's representative, at every committee meeting, and then also being a rainmaker.

Black partners often solve that problem—or attempt to solve it—by taking a wholesale approach: "I'm going to take all of the black associates out for a beer and offer advice to all of them at once." The challenge there is, you need to give very individualized attention at times. Becoming partner is very challenging, because that's kind of the last hurdle, so all the biases, implicit and explicit, come to the table: Are you good enough to be allowed through this last door?

But even once you make it, diversity professionals spend as much time helping partners of color to be successful as they do associates. It is extremely difficult to be successful as a partner in a high-powered law firm today. The demands on you are triple what they were a decade ago in terms of business development, firm citizenship hours, billables. It is overwhelming. It destroys a lot of people personally, including their families.

Law as a profession has been very slow to change around making the balance better for men and women. In terms of people of color, of course, their problems are magnified, even once they make partner—getting clients who are going to give them the business, having the connections they need to truly be successful. They need a sponsor to get them through and help them be successful. If they're not with the right institutional clients, or don't have some relationship that will make them succeed, they will be pushed out the door. So it is not realistic to expect partners of color to mentor every associate of color who comes through the door. Every attorney at the firm needs to be involved in this.

Managing partners at big law firms today need to be seriously concerned about the lack of partners who are Asian—let alone African American and Latino. Any given firm has at most only a handful of partners of color. But there aren't a lot of senior associates of color, either, to move up the ranks. What are the first steps a managing partner should take to address this situation?

Diversity is not the purview of people of color at the firm. It's a management issue. For a firm that is organized, as many are, by departments and practice groups, the development of talent, including talent of color, has to reside with the practice group leaders. And they have to be held accountable. What does that look like as a practical matter? It involves the intentional development of associates from day one. That starts with the summer program, because that's when a young attorney's reputation starts to be established.

Pair your associates of color, especially your black and brown associates, with your strongest-performing associates, not necessarily your senior associates of color, because oftentimes we don't have enough successful models of senior associates of color in our networks to be mentors.

Beyond coaching summer associates, what can managing partners do to fix the leaky pipeline further up the ladder? Let's assume that a law firm now has 50 percent more associates of color coming in the September class than it has ever had. How does the firm hold onto them and help them become partners?

The first step is to redefine what the goal is. Because a lot of young people today will shut down the minute you say, "So that you can become partner." You have to reframe it for them. The goal can't simply be partnership; instead, it's, "This is the beginning of your career in the legal profession. And, by the way, the profession is really small; we all eventually know each other. We all eventually talk. So whether you want to be a partner at Law Firm X, no matter what, as long as you stay in the profession, you're going to be interacting with these people as your peers and as your colleagues, for the rest of whatever your end goal results are. You may not like it here every step of the way, but this is where you chose to be developed." Approaching things from that kind of professional development perspective is going to be more resonant with young associates today than talking to them about making partner.

It's important for diversity professionals to have a very candid conversation with associates very early on about the value proposition—either they want to invest in their careers or they don't. "If you're not working hard, you're not learning and you're not developing relationships, and now you're wasting your time. If you're just here for the paycheck and to pay off a couple of loans and then do the next thing, no problem. Actually, let me know that, so I don't spend a whole lot of time on you, because I don't have a lot of time." I'm focused on partners, on getting our leaders to act right, so I need to know which associates want the value proposition, and then I will help them.

If an associate is not billing a lot of hours, she isn't seeing different types of matters and transactions, she's not learning, not building her deal sheet, then she won't have anything to take with her if she leaves. Associates of color need to ask themselves, "What do you want people to say about you when you're not in the room?" and "What is your professional brand, your personal brand going to be?" If you come to every meeting slouchy and inappropriately dressed, and you're trying not to work that hard, and you're phoning it in, what does that say about you? That's going to carry into everything you do, in every space—future jobs, civic activities, board service, all of it.

Let's assume a firm has a bunch of associates of color who are all attending meetings, making substantive contributions, working late every night, and hitting their hours. They're bright-eyed and bushy-tailed, committed folks, but that still doesn't lead to retention and promotion. What should a firm do structurally, internally,

to make sure those associates have a chance to succeed?

The key thing here is engagement. Retention and promotion are about the mechanics of doing the work. Engagement is the emotional investment.

Senior people at the firms need to talk to young associates of color, and they also need to give them a voice. "Yes, you're doing everything you're supposed to do by our metrics, but are you satisfied? Are you feeling a sense of gratification from your work, from the environment? What could we do better?" And if they feel comfortable getting to the question of authenticity, "Do you feel that you can bring your whole self to work?" Management needs to make an effort to understand the things that are important to associates in their personal lives. A lot of people of color in law firms hide that. They're covering up, and that brings its own psychological burden that can even have a physical toll.

The confidence piece comes up a lot with associates of color on their way out of a firm, or with alumni who have departed, and they finally get that "aha" moment and are able to articulate things like, "Oh, my first two, three years, *this* was what was missing." Often they will focus on the concept of belonging, and the fact that law firms could do a better job on that front.

Engagement is a corporate word that has yet to truly take hold in the legal space. But it's coming, and whether we've said it or not, we know it when we see it. So a managing partner, in addition to saying, "You have the billable hours, and you seem to have the intellectual curiosity around what you're doing," needs to ask, "But where is your heart in this?" That's the engagement piece, because that's what tells someone, "I want to spend more time with you. I want to actually know what you're about."

So the engagement piece is a managing partner saying, "I know you can do the work, because we've already screened you and know that you are intelligent enough to be here. But do you want to be here? Do you have in context, in your heart, how all of this plays out? Because then you will engage and invest in a way that will make me, as managing partner, want to engage and invest in you too."

But one managing partner engaging that way often doesn't cascade down to the rest of the partners and some of the senior associates. The other attorneys kind of say, "Well, that's nice. He does it, and he's got his one or two pet associates." How do we get that to cascade through the firm?

Clients help. But that's an external driver. When you have a partner stewardship problem, and your partners don't care about cultivating the associates—much less going a bit further for those who need specialized support—that's a real management problem.

One strategy is to motivate management through compensation. Most firms could do a lot better in compensating what they really, truly value. Typically, all they compensate is billable hours. Then you have the managing partner saying, "But don't forget engagement, and partner stewardship, and make sure you're making time to do X, Y, and Z," and these partners are like, "I cannot. There are only so many hours in a day. I've got to hit my billable hours. I don't have time for the niceties of making these associates feel better, and they're all entitled and pains anyway." So you have a real motivation problem.

And you have to teach behavior ahead of partnership. Once they're partners and "citizenship" is no longer coming into play, you lose the leverage. Firms have to start earlier, creating a culture where white male senior associates feel as if they should be mentoring and giving feedback to younger associates of color. Whether you feel like doing it or not, if it's tied to your compensation, miraculously, you seem to find a way.

Leadership skills can be exercised at any point in the structure; you don't need a title. We need to be teaching this kind of intentional leadership beginning in law school, right through summer associateships and new hires. "How can I succeed as a black or brown lawyer and make this firm more sensitive to issues of diversity?" Or, "How, as a white partner, can I help folks succeed?" In addition to being more likely to be promoted to partner, attorneys who are asking themselves these intentional kind of leadership questions are more likely to find professional satisfaction.

How do we prepare the high-performing associates to invest in the development of summer associates?

We tell them that it's their job, and they will be held accountable with measurable results. That includes things like: Are you supervising their assignments? Are you making yourself available? Are you checking in with them on how they're doing, not waiting for them to come to you with a question (because that's not going to happen)? And, are you giving transparent, candid, and constructive feedback?

It's very granular. That first assignment, and often the second and third assignments, are critical. Is the firm being very strategic on what work is even assigned? Was there a pre-meeting with the associate before the work was turned in? Did you ask the associate what feedback he got from the partner on that assignment? "Let's talk through that feedback; let's decode what they told you versus what is really being communicated, whether you realize it or not." "Okay, now assignment two, let's do it again." Because assignment two, especially at the summer level, probably doesn't look like the previous assignment.

Are associates who are not associates of color getting that kind of feedback?

Yes, but it's happening more organically. The less perceived difference there is, the more likely that conversation is happening on the way to the elevator. If that associate looks like me, goes to the ballgame with me, went to my undergraduate or law school, I'm more likely to offer advice. You probably have higher expectations of that person also—that person reminds you of yourself.

And by the way, with respect to the conversation with the summer associate of color, what we often have to explain to anyone giving feedback is that the model is not, "Okay, let's all sit at the table, and let's all review the assignment." It's not that formalized. It's a one-on-one conversation on the way to the elevator: "You know, you probably shouldn't have said it that way in that call. Next time try to lower your register a bit. I think you'll command the room a little bit better."

It's two seconds. It's on the way to the elevator, but that's valuable feedback. If you're not even asking me to walk with you to go get coffee on the way to the elevator, I don't get that feedback, because I'm waiting until the end of the summer, when you're going to formally evaluate me. So that's why the relationships matter. Do I have enough rapport with you, where I'm getting these little nuggets just from being with you?

That can work for senior associates, if it's an explicit deliverable that in order for senior associates who supervise the summer associates to ascend, the senior associates have to show some metrics regarding those summer associates coming on as permanent offers. But what can be done to get existing partners on board?

It's not one-size-fits-all. For lockstep firms that don't have structures where you can incentivize with money, you have to figure out other motivators, which often involve personalized professional development plans at the partner level. To the extent that you're asking individual partners to report out on their practices—and also practice groups on the plan for their practice—the partners in each area have to develop a talent pipeline with the aim of increasing diversity as one of its goals. And the plan has to be very specific. It's going to vary for different practice groups: For practice areas like insurance, healthcare, banking, you can use clients to push, because partners are going to be really responsive. In equity, they're getting there, but they're not where the others are because there isn't the external pressure.

We're all familiar with the study where partners judged the content of legal memos differently when they knew the race of the associates who had written them. How transparent should firms

be, in light of this? Should we tell associates, "You will be judged differently if you're an associate of color than if you're a white associate"?

There are two schools of thought here. The first school is to share the information with the partners, but not with the associates of color. The partners are driven by data and analysis. The biggest successes we've had on the diversity front are from showing partners the data. For example, saying to a partner in a given practice area, "The firm now has a very high representation of senior women. This is the percentage for your group, and this is the percentage of all senior women you're promoting to partner. There's an abysmal gap." And they're like, "Oh, that smacks of sexism and bias." Yes. Yes, it does. So data really moves people.

Associates of color are more likely to react differently to the same data. They don't have the agency to change the culture, and they're more likely to respond with, "What do you want me to do with that information? That's awful, so I'm out of here." When we have shared that study with associates, it has had that impact: "Oh, so I'm doomed. I might as well leave." On the other hand, what it also has done is begin to build awareness around, "Here's the truth of the matter. You are being judged differently." And step one for achieving change is creating awareness.

Step two is, now let's get some tips and some tools for managing that bias when we confront it. In theory, this creates an environment where it's safe to say: "We all have the same language, we all have the same baseline information, which is, this is not a meritocracy. This is not an even playing field. And so, you know, is bias coming into this conversation?" We're in the early days of this, but people are starting to say, "Is this challenging for you to give me this feedback because I'm a woman? Because I want the feedback more than I want you to feel comfortable. So I need to hear it. Where am I?" Partners are hearing that same conversation, so it creates, in theory, a common baseline. But we're not there yet. It's still aspirational.

If associates of color don't have the information, they also think they're being judged on the same basis. Then they look at their white counterparts and think, "I do everything she does, but I don't get invited to go to golf. I don't get it." And that creates a different problem.

On the whole, we're finding allyship in everyone having the same information. We're now seeing white male junior associates saying things like, "Why are you validating my point more than what that senior woman of color said? She just made that same point." We're teaching allyship, but it's a process. At this point, it's not clear that any senior associates are going to state, "I am an ally." But what we do know and what we are seeing is that the men are more attuned to, "I'm talking over her. You know what? That's exactly what they told us about in the training. Let me step back, she has the floor." It's difficult, and it's early days. So, we're certainly not yet saying, "It works!"

On the recruitment piece, the study that says résumés with black-sounding names don't generate interviews at the same rates doesn't ring true with current experience. These days, at least at some firms, there's such a focus on increasing diversity that the fact that you have an Asian- or Latino- or African American–sounding name, or that you were a member of BALSA *is* noticed, and it's definitely not a deterrent for hiring.

We know about 80 percent of first-years will flame out and are ultimately not going to make it. But you'll be great ambassadors for us at your law school, you may go on to work for our clients, you may be at the next Facebook, or whatever, even if you don't stay. We *want* the diversity coming in. Now we need to translate our recruiting efforts into tangible progress on the retention and promotion front.

Firms might also want diversity of a certain type— the type of diversity that goes to certain schools or has a certain pedigree.

In smaller cities, firms not only have to attract law students of color to the city, but also expand their recruitment pool. Too often their recruitment issues are compounded because they're still hiring law review students with a certain complexion, from a very finite number of schools. Firms in the bigger cities for the most part have moved beyond that, at least the large firms. And so the challenge is more in going beyond the top fourteen law schools. Or not looking at Howard as a diversity initiative. We're recruiting at Howard because it's an excellent law school. It's not part of a diversity initiative.

In terms of getting the partners to behave differently, it is rare for a straight white male partner to refuse a direct request from a diversity professional, such as: "Listen, this is the lived experience of this associate of color who is having a really difficult time, and I need someone like you who has the attributes, the connections, the voice, to help him. Would you please help?"

They feel flattered to be asked on some level, and the fact that a high-achieving associate of color is having a hard time also flies in the face of their notion of a meritocracy. They don't want that meritocracy narrative to be a myth, so when you directly point out to them that the associate is "doing everything that everybody else is doing, and this is still the experience they're having, will you help?" they say yes. And that's what we spend a lot of our time doing on behalf of individual lawyers—getting them that more senior person to be their sponsor.

Is talking to a straight male white partner like that a relatively new thing?

No, we've been doing that for years. And we will have to do it tomorrow.

So we all need to do that?

Absolutely. With only one partner of color at a firm of, say, three hundred partners, associates can't expect their mentors and sponsors to look like them. And 299 partners can't expect one partner of color to mentor every associate of color. So even if a firm has the best chairman, that's also only one person. Whether you're a national or international firm, one person only has so much bandwidth. So we absolutely need to get the partners to engage in this way.

Is it more compelling to make the business case or the moral case for getting white partners to feel like they have to champion diversity in the firm?

The business case often doesn't work. If a firm happens to have a client who cares about this, then your business case works, but other than that, it doesn't matter what science we show partners about how diverse, engaged teams do better in X, Y, and Z ways. It's in one ear and out the other.

It ultimately comes down to the moral case, and debunking the idea of a meritocracy. And for many people, you have the challenge of, when you present the business case, it offends them. They only want to hear the moral case, so it's tricky. To me, the only business case is, "Look, these are our clients who care about this. You are trying to break into the space, and there are 25 percent and rising general counsels of color. They are kicking firms off of their panels, throwing them out of the room for showing up with all–white male pitch teams, yet you continue to do it." That's your smartest business case argument. And that's as far as you usually can go.

What are the most creative and successful things you've seen law firms do to increase opportunities for folks of color?

Formal programs are the most effective. Anyone who says, "Oh, formal programs don't work. It has to be organic," is lying. For women and for people of color, you by and large need formal programs, including sponsorship programs. You have to force the interaction. And not mass-scale programs—very individualized ones. What are a given associate's goals and aspirations? Are they in the right practice area? Who within the practice would be the best partner to shepherd this associate's career? Firms need to be incredibly intentional and high touch in terms of every single pairing. It's not scalable.

Firms actually need a playbook for that. As smart and savvy as partners are, when it comes to difference, they're extremely uncomfortable. So basic things that you would think you could just run through in a conversation like, "Ask the associates of color what they're interested in. What have they worked on?" Somehow the basic stuff goes out the window. For generally articulate people, it's shocking that you have to be prescriptive with that stuff, but that's what works.

Number one in the playbook for partners is "forgive mistakes." Focus on the good intentions, because there's not a lot of resilience. Be a coach and not a critic. Making a mistake should not be a young associate of color's undoing; it should be an opportunity for a partner or senior associate to teach.

Associates need to demonstrate that they want to be coached, and then we need to ask partners, "Are you coaching, or are you criticizing and labeling from day one ('she's horrible, she's a disaster') based on the one assignment that a new associate happened to mess up?" By labeling people this way in talks with their colleagues, partners think they're just being conversational, but what they're doing is creating a brand for the associate that's preventing her from having future opportunities. All that the other partners remember about this conversation is, "Oh, I heard that she was a disaster. And I'm supposed to take her on my next matter?"

That's part of the weakness of law firms: because they rarely have formal work allocation systems and managers, there are seemingly endless opportunities for bias, explicit and implicit, to creep in.

What can young associates of color do to improve their law firm experiences?

Like it or not, the disproportionate burden of bridging difference falls on the young attorneys of color. And that impacts the numbers, because the number of talented students who are willing to ask for feedback and to create relationships is dwindling. It's a generational issue.

We coach associates of color with their side of the equation: When you're asked to attend something, go! I don't care if you like golf or not. That's not the point.

You have access that you're not going to be offered again if you turn this opportunity down. You've got to be engaged. You don't have to go to every social event, but you have to demonstrate that "this isn't my 9 to 5, or even my 9 to 9. I'm part of this culture." You at least have to demonstrate that you drank the Kool-Aid, even if you didn't swallow.

From the summer associate's perspective, you also have to tell them that, although it's not always intuitive, the onus is on them to create the safe space. It shouldn't have to be this way, but at the end of the day this is their career. They have to work harder to invite that feedback across difference.

So in preparing law students for, say, Early Interview Week, should they be told that one of the law firms' filters is, "Are you a self-starter? Are you someone who can develop that relationship?"

That is one of the competencies firms are interviewing for. They're asking competency-based behavioral interview questions. Absolutely.

We've talked about metrics for the partners and their compensation package. Should we have metrics for the associates of color? Should we be saying to them when they walk in the door, "You went to that funky little diversity session at law school," or "We did a training for you," and then debrief them in some way to see what they walked away with after that conversation?

Firms have sort of been doing that, where someone from professional development will say, "Oh, yes, we have career plans, and that's how we measure if you're developing at the right pace." But now we also have diversity professionals following up after the trainings, saying, "Here's what that looks like in practice. If you're going to hear a lunchtime speaker at a different firm, and you walk out of that room without three new contacts, then you missed an opportunity."

Will you find that written, per se, anywhere? Probably not. But do we know, "Hey guys, you don't just go to the event for the event's sake. It's also, 'How many people did you meet?' Because that's expanding your network. And why do you need to expand your network? Because you know you don't want to be at this firm forever. Or even if you do, knowing somebody at that other firm can help you when you need to make it rain."

Associates who may one day want to be public defenders, or go to prosecutors' offices, need to think about the brand they're making for themselves. Who's going to write your recommendation? If you're thinking in your second year that you've been under the radar—it happens all the time—and you decide, "I want to work in the U.S. Attorney's office," well, who is going to vouch for you? You don't know anybody! So, building a brand and a reputation are critical.

Some of these things are very specific to associates of color at private law firm practice, but many are things that anybody starting out in the legal profession needs to be aware of.

Is there a greater role for law schools to play in preparing students of color for work in big law?

We really, really need law schools to do more to get their students and junior associates showing up with much more professional maturity. Maybe it's the trend of young people going straight from undergrad to grad school with no work experience, but generational attitudes toward professionalism in the workplace are one of the biggest challenges. The level of entitlement that students are showing up with is astounding. They seem not to appreciate that law firms are competitive businesses. Firm members should not be wasting time teaching this to adults, to professionals. An associate's number one job is to make somebody else's life easier. And they do not get this. There is a real role for law schools here.

Besides teaching professional maturity, what else can law schools do?

Possibly as a result of eight years of an Obama administration, students of color are graduating today without a clear sense of the professional obstacles they will face on the basis of their race. We are shocked when we sit across from a black or brown person and have to explain, "You're not being judged on the same standard." It's a reality check. They don't seem to understand that—not at all.

The mere fact that we're having to repeat the old saw, "You have to work—forget twice—three or four times as hard to get to the same place," is shocking. They don't see that. At all. And having it explained to them hurts their feelings. It is amazing that this seems not to have come up for them before. Students are affronted when we say that to them. And they're argumentative: "What are you talking about?"

We say to them. "To be clear, I'm not saying that this is the way things ought to be, or that this is how we want them to be here, but until we get to where we're trying to go, this is what you're dealing with today."

They're ready to walk out the door.

Resilience and grit are key competencies for success at a law firm, and law schools could do more to help develop this. How does a young associate of color deal with the steady stream of microaggressions? Because guess what? We're not changing the culture in the next few minutes. You work here now, and things aren't changing in the time frame that you would like them to, so, let's focus more on "How are you going to survive in the now?" And that's about resiliency. The younger the associate, the less and less resiliency. Or at least the more impatience. I'm not sure if that's generational: "I don't have to do this. I can go do nonprofit work, then I'll work for a virtual law firm for a few years, and then maybe I'll plug back in . . ."

One of the things that happens with new law students of color is they hear something in that first week of class, that white professor says something that they perceive as racist, and they shut down. And the corollary happens in a law firm as well. That's where the resilience comes in, because they're like, "You mean the world's not fair?"

Every first-year law student of color getting ready for the summer program at a firm would likely benefit from this kind of discussion during the spring semester. For summer associates who have finished their first summer at a firm and are about to get their callback offer in the fall, a refresher discussion might come right beforehand. Third-year law students and associates would likely benefit from a session in the summer, before they start studying for the bar, so that when they go to the firm in September or October, they're coming in with this knowledge.

Should students of color be meeting and having conversations with advisers at law schools before they start summer associate positions about what it means to not only survive but also thrive in corporate law firm culture?

Absolutely. It probably takes both law schools and diversity professionals at the law firms, though it's a delicate dance in a firm. You can do it with *all* the associates, but the message gets diluted a bit. Other places where those kinds of conversations can happen is through affinity groups, networks, and relevant special interest organizations and centers at law schools. Affinity groups in particular offer perhaps the safest spaces. (Affinity groups are support organizations within the firm that focus on supporting under-represented groups, such as lawyers of color.)

I think there's a general conversation just in terms of a tutorial that should happen for all law students: "This is what it means to work in a corporate law firm." I think when they arrive on a firm's doorstep, the firm should have another conversation from that particular firm's perspective: "In general, this is the code of conduct."

But then, in a safer space such as an affinity group, advisers can really drill down: "Here's the real deal. Like it or don't like it, but this is the real deal."

Professional maturity, reality check with resilience—anything else law schools can do better?

On the management side, there is just no teaching around the business of running a law firm. We never

firm, are just not going to have a good experience
ey don't come in with an awareness of that.

at role can affinity groups play in profession-
development, beyond just the "let's all go out
drinks" social role?

netimes, the most critical feedback about someone's
rk comes through affinity groups. On the issue of
veloping a brand early, either as an asset or a disas-
, for example, there are instances where an associ-
e who is not being given work asks her supervisors,
ow am I doing?" and the answer is "Oh, fine, fine,"
en though everyone around her seems busier than
ie is. In this case, members of an affinity group who
re more senior, and perhaps are friends with the peo-
le who have judged that person harshly, can get to
he bottom of it. And then they can either press it upon
he supervisor who had the bad experience to give that
eedback, or say to that associate, "No. Everyone else
s getting assignments, so clearly there's an issue. Go
oack to the senior associate or the partner and tell

had it in law school; we work with partners who also
never had it. So when we're asking for more enlight-
ened diversity policies, we're generally not speaking
with trained managers. We recognize that this isn't
going to be solved immediately, but it's on the wish list.

The fact that a law firm is a business, and "here's
what the client expects," also needs to be a part of law
school curricula. "Here are the professional standards
that go with delivering that client service. You're
not here just to better yourself or pursue knowledge
around X, Y, and Z. There is a business case for why
you're even here." Reminding law students of this context would help all young associates, and in particular
associates of color, who may be the first in their families to hold this kind of job.

Let's start at the beginning. It's a client service business. So, when you don't answer your phone on Satur-
day, that's a problem. The client wants to know right
now, "What's the answer to this?" More training about
professionalism would be very helpful. Young associates of color already face a lot of questions about their

own level of competence; the issue of impostor syndrome is real. The more explicit we can be about expectations, standards of behavior, and so on, the better.

We particularly see the tendency toward self-doubt with a lot of black male associates. What they needed to do to survive and be considered good enough derails them when it's time to go from this point to the next. We have to, in general, help them understand who they are and how they're going to be seen, and then ask, What is the environment they're going to encounter, and how do they navigate it? How do they adapt in a way that is authentic for them?

It's not just black men obviously. You know, it's things as basic as knowing whether you are what Adam Grant calls a work-life segregator, in contrast to a work-life aggregator. If you are a work-life segregator, you are not going to survive in a law firm. When you go on vacation, if you're not willing to review a box of documents for about three hours in the morning of one of your vacation days, you're not going to make

it. There are plenty of people who should be able to check out."

They're not interested in the me minute you're in this place, for as lor place, learning, billing, building you vating relationships." It's not for them determine that sooner rather than la be miserable? Why come and waste time, and the partners' time, and cre for lawyers of color? Law schools can h neys of color understand that the way live beyond you. These days we see les legacy and reputation than we're used t ferent generationally.

We can't change this generation. The push the culture forward in good ways firms are having to adapt, from our ph to how we do a lot of things. But certain aren't going to change in the short term. associates of color, if they actually do war

them, good, bad, ugly, you want to hear it." So this unfiltered piece is a unique role for an affinity group.

Affinity groups can also do a lot of programming around some of the "soft skills," to reinforce the general programming that's done for summer associates and new arrivals. They can more intentionally lay out all of what is typically communicated informally—things that may not be intuitive and that young associates of color may not be aware of. When a partner asks a new associate to set up a call, he will not give you the ten steps involved. Somehow, you're supposed to know what those are. So what does that look like: the conference room, the room layout—even the refreshments—the whole bit. They just expect you to put it together. But unless you've done it before, or you have someone who can pull your coat and say, "This is what that means," you may not know. Decoding is critical. Young associates of color need law firm culture decoded for them.

It's also a two-way street. Partners need to be introduced to other cultures as well. It's important to try to level the comfort quotient. So, for instance, at one firm, the Asian affinity group pointed out, "We celebrate all of these other cultures, but Diwali is very important in our culture, and how come the firm doesn't have a Diwali celebration?"

And the answer to that was and should be, "Let's have a Diwali celebration." And so now, that's that firm's favorite celebration. And it offers a different kind of opportunity to create access and comfort. For the associate, it's, "Now I know you outside of just doing this deal, or writing this memo for you." And for the partner, it's, "We tried these new foods together, and I learned a little bit more about a culture that perhaps I wouldn't necessarily have access to." So there's a role for affinity groups to bring things like this to the attention of the firm: "We want to be celebrated too. We want you to understand who we are, and this is a big deal in our culture."

Even inside the group, there are differences to be appreciated and learned from. The South Asians will say, "Well, I celebrate something very differently than the East Asians." So, the goal is to create small opportunities for all those nuances to come to light, even in the context of a very fast-paced, stressful environment: "Can't we have lunch, and can't we have a quick little orientation about what Diwali is? It's celebrated differently depending on where you're from. And then let's eat; we all need lunch."

In the current social and political times, young people of color in particular need truly safe spaces to decompress and talk about what's happening. Affinity groups can provide that. One of the hardest things is just showing up every day in the face of an administration that appears to thwart civil rights, and everybody just going about their business. After the presidential election, it was the affinity groups that got together and had a very emotional, very difficult call, where everyone was able to just vent, and then put themselves back together. Women partners of color were crying in those meetings. So many associates were so emotional, and when you had the shootings of Alton Sterling and Philando Castile within days of each other, people were weeping. The affinity groups provided an incredibly important resource, and there would have been no other way to have that conversation or provide that support to the members.

How would you characterize the role of diversity professional at a law firm?

Diversity professionals bring healing to a space that has no healing. We have commonsense conversations. We help the partners with the interpersonal aspects of the job: "You're brilliant, but you really don't know how to just have this simple conversation." No, they don't, because law school training, by and large, doesn't teach you to be thinking about managing people, reading the room, all of those things. Diversity professionals let the partners know, "Hey, I'm here to help you. I know how difficult your life is. How can I make it better?" And, to the young lawyers, they say, "I know all the pressures. What's a challenge for you? What doors can I help open?"

These roles are fairly new to law firms in the last two decades, and now they are exploding. We work to find out what inspires people, and then help them figure out the point of working for a law firm in light of their personal goals: "Why should I do this if I could do all these other things?" It's not for everybody—pleasing these partners night and day to get the value out of the experience. But it is for some people, so helping them understand what they can get out of it is very powerful.

The motivation is different for different people. For some attorneys of color, it's very much tied to civil rights—that's why a lot of black young women go into the profession. We try to get people to see the big picture, that these institutions impact the entire society. These people you are learning from and developing relationships with—they know people in power all over the world. And if you show them that you are present at the firm, living and breathing it, and on their team to help provide the service that they're tasked with providing, they will in turn give you A, B, and C. You may not understand that now, but you will understand it later.

We also share our personal stories to let young associates of color know that this stint in a law firm, however long you're there, can be socioeconomically transformative for entire families. The experience can change the whole trajectory of a life and a career—just who you know, who you can pick up the phone and call, who you can ask to help someone else. One of our most important roles is getting new associates to understand that they're wasting such valuable time if they don't conduct themselves in a way that maximizes the opportunity. Oftentimes, they don't get it, they can't see it, until it's too late—when they're struggling in that job and don't have the referral.

We still have to advertise that we're here, and what it is that we actually offer. Often associates don't know how to use us. And so we find out on the back end, when someone is about to get the unhappy message that it's time for them to exit. That is always a source of frustration for me: "Why didn't you come to me sooner?" They come to do their exit interview, and at that point, when it's too late, they ask themselves the same question: "Why didn't I come to you sooner?"

How rare a creature are you all? And are there folks who have your title but don't have your philosophy? Is there, within your business, a consistency of the kind of ideas you've discussed?

Most of us are drawn to this work because we care and want to make a difference for associates and for firms, so we get down in the weeds and do this work. At some firms, diversity professionals are really hampered. They don't get resources; their bar association has them just focus on events, externalities, but not the people. At some firms, the position is very client-facing: they just want to check a box for the clients, and they want somebody who's very visible.

Students of color evaluating a firm need to really look and make sure there's someone in the role to begin with. And if there is a diversity professional, how much staff and support does that person have? What's their voice? The reporting structure actually matters. When diversity staff are reporting through

other administrative departments, it truly hampers
what they can achieve. That's a signal about how
effective they can possibly be. By contrast, if that person reports directly to the chair and the management
committee, not just the partners who run the diversity
initiative, that's a sign that they truly have influence
and can move the needle on your behalf.

The firm's diversity professional should report to
partners and should be part of the hiring process.
Those are subtle signals about where diversity and
inclusion is valued.

At a law school, the diversity staff should report
directly to the dean. If they're reporting to anybody
other than the dean, that sends a message about the
value of the role.

**The majority of diversity professionals are
people of color. They themselves have to live
through not only the microaggressions that
happen to everyone of color at a big law firm,
but also the treatment typically accorded peo-**

**ple at the firm who don't have their own book
of business. How do you make the case that you
add value to the firm?**

If you're doing diversity work at a firm where you also
practice, it's especially challenging. You know all the
firm's dirty laundry—what they really care about,
don't care about—and you have to come from a place of
integrity. You have to shift them to the right place, but
also be honest and candid, and that is really challenging when you are doing this work at the place where
you grew up.

You may not be as valued when you grow up through
the system. They want the bright and shiny thing from
that firm over there that they really admire. I think
you're more likely to be taken for granted, and people
aren't really able to see your value separate and apart
from when you practiced at the firm. Plus, you didn't
become a partner, and who doesn't want to become a
partner, right? So they're already making an assessment about you.

On the other hand, the fact that you initially practiced at the firm and then changed gears—not because you were pushed out, but because you made a conscious choice—can work in your favor. "You were once one of us, right?" At a firm where they think they're the best of the best, the fact that you were even in the sandbox with them counts for something. "We've seen your work before, which is what ultimately is important to us, so we'll give you access to certain things." At certain firms, anyway. This can also lead to blind spots, though, because at some point you drank the Kool-Aid the same way they have. So you may have a tendency to think, "No, that can't happen because that's not how we do things here." So it can cut both ways.

As our peers start graduating out of the firm, our role has changed also. To that first-year associate coming in now, we're seen as senior people, with all this knowledge and wisdom, instead of someone they went to law school with.

For those of us who practiced first, we definitely benefit from credibility when we're talking to the younger associates: "Oh, I've been there, I've done that." For the partners, though, it's more like, "We already know what her biases are," or, "That's just her. She's been saying the same thing for the past ten years." Hearing it from a new voice might sometimes be more effective.

Being able to put together a greatest-hits list of how associates of color have succeeded—and that doesn't necessarily mean attaining partnership—is very valuable. Summer associates will talk about the "Go" plan and the "Stay" plan, and they always need to have both. Either plan may be sitting on the front burner, but both need to be in place. Diversity professionals need to be pretty transparent with young associates, and the professionals themselves need to have a reality check, asking, "Am I committing professional suicide here?" Because, you know, we'll tell the emperor he has no clothes. Certainly, there are presiding partners who are genuinely deeply committed and want to do better. So it's important to know your audience.

There have to be metrics. That's really how we validate what we do and determine this was or wasn't successful. It's built into everything we do. But then people tend to rely only on the data points to govern what comes next, and that's where, depending on your organization, risk is either tolerated or not.

So, for instance, Howard University is not a risky conversation for us because we have enough metrics, data points that say, "When we recruited from Howard, we did well there." So the next step isn't like, "Okay, so let's sell Howard to the partnership." It's, "This works. Next question." There doesn't have to become a discussion around that.

On the other hand, people will be quick to say, "It's a meritocracy. We don't really need that diversity program anymore." And so you phase out something that in retrospect was really important. It turns out that other things were going on there besides what you could measure in terms of netting the result you were looking for. There have been times where, to our detriment, we've relied too heavily on the metrics.

A good example of that is how we've utilized associates. We've had to do a lot of consciousness-raising about the way we start conversations around work assignments. We typically begin by looking at billable hours and how time is being spent at work at the start of the conversation.

But really, the conversation should be about the quality of those hours. Billable hours, especially for the junior classes, seem to offer an easy way of trying to gauge if the seventy or eighty new associates in one year at the firm are progressing at roughly the same pace. The numbers will tell you one story. And if there are large differentials in the numbers, that's something to be addressed immediately. But even if the numbers look similar, you need to unpack the numbers and understand what they mean. Are the associates getting the type of work that is suitable for their level? Are they gaining increasing responsibility? Do they have exposure to clients?

Have you seen other innovative things that you think would move the needle, in terms of the success of associates of color and their promotion

through the ranks to partner, that made you think, "I wish I could do that"?

Quotas. Because to really cut through the bias, ultimately, you have to force the firms to have people of color. When people in positions of power are pushed to go outside their comfort zone, they almost always end up saying, "Oh, I'm shocked. People of color actually were successful." But you have to force them to do it. The problem is, quotas are too stigmatizing to those you would be promoting. It doesn't matter if you're a woman or a person of color, a whole bunch of people in the firm think you only got there because you're a woman or a person of color.

The people who get those positions are just devastated by any suggestion that there was a quota system in place. There are many people I've helped a lot, and they're aware of it, but once they've made partner, and I'm being effusive and congratulatory, they can barely bring themselves to acknowledge me or say thanks. At that point, they're feeling more like, "Please don't associate with me" or "Why are you here?" Until they need you. Until they face the next set of challenges as partner.

The entire structure needs to reflect the firm's value: performance management, compensation, and accountability. No matter what creative or software-driven plan any given firm has, there has not been enough innovation in terms of better ways to measure talent. How do you really judge potential? How do you develop talent? How do you not write people off based on that first or second assignment? And, at the management level, how do you reward a partner for developing potential in the young attorneys of color? Until we can really have that honest conversation, it will continue to be a biased system.

Senior associates and partners need to be trained to give meaningful feedback, not, "Oh, well, you know, she did okay." What do I do with "okay," in terms of measuring her potential? Lawyers in particular are conscious of what they're putting in writing about someone's performance. The result can be a really sanitized version of "She's great" or "She did a good job." What does that mean? How do I advance her in the areas where she excelled? Where do I give constructive criticism about how to get better? We're very reluctant to give honest feedback, because law firms don't really know how to develop talent. That's a problem across the industry.

Fortune 100 companies generally identify what they call "high performers" pretty early on, and then they structure quite individualized development plans for them. That doesn't seem to translate into law firms.

Law firms don't identify "high performers" or individuals with "high potential" early in their careers the way Fortune 100 companies do. Those companies will target those high performers as a group of the next set of leaders and will structure both learning and work opportunities to develop their skills and to prepare them to advance in the companies. In law firms, the trajectory to partnership is a bit more haphazard, in that it is typically more subjective and individualized. There is also often no explicit recognition of race and ethnicity in thinking about the partnership path.

We're trying, but often we're working without the buy-in of the people actually writing the reviews. Diversity professionals know what needs to happen. If a firm has eighteen black associates, the diversity professional typically has a pretty good sense of where each one of those people stands. They're able to decode. *"He said I did fine."* "Hmm, you didn't do fine. Let me give you some feedback on 'fine.'"

The people who have been seasoned and have seen this happen over a number of years know how to be influential in changing the image or brand of a young associate, helping that person understand what the next assignment should be so that they grow and develop as a lawyer. We know how to do it, but the firm is still using the same performance review system from twelve years ago. We know that doesn't work.

But it can be dangerous to try and identify high performers early in associates' careers at law firms, because, as the saying goes, "Good lawyers are not born, they're made." The person who is mentoring them, who's really grasping what they are about and where they fit in, can make all the difference. Oftentimes, they are in the wrong practice group, and they are so bored by the drudgery of it all that they're not performing. But in the right practice group, they would be stars and the clients would love them. There can also be a disconnect where the clients will love an associate, but the partners are like, "Eh. You know, I don't think so highly of him."

So a system catered to stars is tricky, and coming up with a plan for high performers can be rife with bias to begin with. There are certain competencies that are clear from the get-go: a young associate of color has the drive, they're handing in quality work, and so on. They just don't need a lot of assistance; they're kind of acting like a partner from the beginning. For those people it is clear, and the goal is to get them on the track and make sure they don't go anywhere.

But then there's that other young person where, had

you invested the time and effort, her potential could have grown. It could have gotten her to the right place. She would be overlooked in a system designed to identify stars from day one. And it's with people who will blossom with the right guidance that we'll ultimately get the numbers we're looking for. Because law firm culture can be so foreign to them, black and brown associates often need high-touch, individualized professional development plans—not just for the high performers, but for every single person.

Compensation and accountability are also key pieces of an infrastructure designed to encourage diversity. A firm may be on top of who's performed well, who's performing average, who's falling behind, but the management team is having the same conversation every two weeks with the partners: Did you give that person work? Did you give that person a review? Did you get that person feedback? And, generally, the answer is the same. "Well, we missed each other," or, "Well, we'll schedule it next week." One partner can't force another partner to do something. Maybe if you're a senior partner and that junior partner's working on your matter, you might have more influence, but it's an inherent problem of partnerships. The CEO at a Fortune 500 company says, "This is what we're doing," and that's what everyone does.

For attorneys of color to succeed in law firms, they need explicit advice; ongoing support, mentorship, and sponsorship; and professional development. They need safe spaces where they can vent and get honest feedback. And they need to be given a voice at the table and a sense of belonging. And it's a two-way street: the more the partners and managers know about you, the more you can explain your point of view.

The Playbook

*What Law Firms and
Law Schools Need to
Consider When Thinking
About Diversity in the
Legal Profession
(And an Important Read
for Law Students Interested
in Law Firms as Well!)*

THIS PLAYBOOK WAS DESIGNED TO BENEFIT SEVERAL groups. For law firms, it identifies the basic steps they can take not only to diversify their ranks but also to create institutional structures; compensation schemes; and recruitment, training, retention, and promotion policies that reflect a commitment to diversity, inclusion, and equity.

For law schools, and particularly law school placement offices, this playbook offers guidance in preparing students of color for the realities and expectations of big law practice. Even those law schools that understand the problem of diversity in big law have done far too little to prepare law students of color for their summer and entry-level experiences at law firms. Partners, academics, and diversity professionals agree that some preparation—in advance of both the all-important summer associate experience and the full-time associate position—would greatly improve the odds of success for law students of color.

The playbook is also a resource for law students and associates of color. When law students of color enter a firm as summer associates or as new associates, they often have nowhere to turn for insider advice about the steps they need to take to succeed. Unlike their white counterparts, they typically do not have family members who have been associates or partners in law firms. And mentors—especially mentors of color—can be hard to come by. So guidance on the steps they need to take to identify mentors and attract sponsors is key to their success. In addition, to thrive in the law firm environment, students must have an understanding of the factors that foster and preserve a good reputation—professionalism; collegiality; and rigorous, high-quality work—and that understanding is most commonly acquired through explicit instruction. The playbook contains specific lessons that might better position law students of color for their summer and postgraduate law firm experiences, lessons that are particularly valuable as the worlds they are about to enter are often fraught with institutional challenges and biases that can undermine their success.

Finally, the playbook hopes to address white law students, associates, and partners—an audience routinely ignored in diversity and inclusion conversations. The focus of diversity and inclusion initiatives is often on people of color—what they can do to adapt and adjust to an environment where they are the minority. But diversity and inclusion are important values for white lawyers as well. The world in which white lawyers are practicing has become more diverse, and they need to understand how to navigate an environment where their perspectives will not necessarily control the experience of people of color or lead to the best advice for them. For this audience, the playbook provides guidance about practicing effective allyship with law students and associates of color.

LAW FIRMS

Being committed to racial diversity begins with an appreciation that diversity is not just a nicety or even simply a moral necessity. It is also a business imperative. Firm leadership needs to articulate and demonstrate that diversity and inclusion are key planks in the business and financial strategy of the firm, making clear that the success of the firm depends on its ability to embrace diversity in its operations.

Buy-in for diversity and inclusion at the top of the firm signals the seriousness of the commitment and the recognition that all leaders within the firm bear responsibility. To that end, law firms can do a number of things to demonstrate a commitment to racial diversity and, in particular, helping to shape a firm climate that reflects and demonstrates thoughtfulness and appropriate sensitivity to race. Some of the recommended actions are structural in nature, while others are operational. But all demonstrate an immediate commitment to the issues at hand. Each of the actions outlined below should flow from a genuine and sustained commitment to the goal of improving racial diversity and developing an atmosphere that allows racially diverse employees to thrive and succeed.

Develop a year-over-year report card on firm-wide diversity goals and efforts.

Most law firms have undertaken some efforts and initiatives to advance the goal of diversity and inclusion. This is, of course, an important first step. But having these efforts in place without assessing whether the firm is actually moving the needle on diversity is little more than window-dressing. What is needed is a regular assessment of those efforts with an eye to identifying what is working, what is not, and what can be changed as part of the discipline of pushing the firm to make progress. What follows are recommendations on steps that firms can take in this process:

Conduct an annual audit.

- As an initial step, hire an external entity with expertise in organizational planning and racial diversity to conduct a rigorous assessment of the current state of affairs. Such an audit should provide a menu of reforms that the firm can undertake to enhance its efforts or address chronic problem areas.

- Thereafter, the firm can determine progress by conducting an annual internal review of their hiring, retention, and promotion as they apply to increasing diversity.

Hire and empower racial diversity professionals.

- Racial diversity professionals should report directly to the managing partner or to the management committee of the firm to signal the importance of the position and to enable faster adoption of recommendations.
- Provide an adequate budget for this position.
- Schedule annual meetings with diversity professionals for all employees of the law firm.
- Ensure that diversity professionals have vis-

attrition of that staff as a part of the targeting and monitoring of demographic growth.

Provide hiring committees with training to identify potential avenues of bias in the hiring process.

- Establish a diverse slate of interviewers.
- Ask all candidates the same questions in the interview portion of the hiring process.
- Use clear evaluation criteria.
- Ask each member of the committee to articulate in writing why he or she selected a particular candidate.

Embed a diversity and inclusion focus in the summer associate program.

The summer associate program is a critical point of entry for the firm. Most firms recognize that they are assessing the talent and fit of summer associates through their summer programs, and that those programs also offer the firm a chance to market themselves and differentiate themselves from competitors.

ibility within the wider organization by having them work directly with the executive committee.

- Give diversity professionals authority to develop firm-wide initiatives; identify trainings, seminars, and speakers for the firm; and engage experts to help the firm develop a more inclusive culture.

Mandate racial diversity training for all personnel.

- Require that senior leadership within the firm attend such trainings.
- Require senior leadership to make clear that issues of diversity affect all lawyers within the firm.
- Provide trainings to address issues such as microaggressions, implicit and explicit bias, and the business case for racial and gender diversity.

*Establish organizational goals for
diversity and inclusion.*

- As with other business goals, firm leadership
  should articulate its expectations on progress
  for diversity and inclusion.
- Goals should include creating formal sponsorship programs and creating an annual diversity assessment for the organization as a whole.

*Include racial diversity as part of per-
formance management and compensation.*

- Establish as a performance criterion the extent to which the lawyer both promotes diversity and inclusion and embodies those values.
- Include diversity and inclusion as performance
  metrics for advancement within the firm.

*Take specific steps to increase inclusion
at points of entry into the firm.*

- Ensure that, as gatekeepers at the principal
  points of entry into law firms, summer and

permanent hiring committees are made ι
a diverse set of lawyers.
- Provide committees with education
  training on diversity in the area of rec
  ing and the ways bias is manifested ir
  process.
- Provide recruiting staff with diversity
  ing as well as training on interviewin;
  practices.
- Provide committees with a clear m
  statement clarifying their operational
  egy for hiring summer interns and ;
  nent hires.
- Clearly spell out metrics for summ
  entry-level associate hiring and inclι
  tors that are less subjective and clear
  tifiable and measurable.
- Make hiring a diverse set of candida
  of the metrics for success for each con
- Systematically measure increases
  creases in staff of color as well as

If a law firm is going to offer a full-time position to a summer associate, they will do so during or at the end of the student's second summer of law school. This system creates an imperative for the summer associate to make a positive impression during that second summer experience. Reputational development begins with those first critical assignments.

(Although the reputation the summer associate builds is crucial, this is just the beginning phase of building a professional brand. Because so much time elapses between an employment offer after the second summer and the full-time associate's start date following her third year of law school, she cannot simply rest on that summer reputation but rather will need to continue to build her brand when she becomes a permanent employee. In essence, a summer associate is starting over again when she starts as a full-time associate.)

Law firms should also understand that the summer associate program provides an opportunity to demonstrate their commitment to diversity and willingness to

invest in the success of young lawyers of color. A failure
to focus on diversity and inclusion in the development
and implementation of the summer associate program
will likely result in a racially divergent and less supportive experience for law students of color. Shaping
the summer so that it serves as a positive growth experience for all summer associates, including associates
of color, requires conscious thought and preparation.
What follows are recommendations for embedding a
diversity and inclusion focus in the summer associate
program:

*Conduct training on cross-racial mentoring before the
summer program begins.*

- Conduct mandatory instruction on mentoring
  for supervising associates and partners who
  expect to participate in summer associate
  programs.
- Create incentives that reward supervising
  attorneys for mentoring in the firm. Options

may include bonuses for supervising associates and partners or adjusting expectations for billable-hour totals for the summer.

- Survey summer associates at the end of the summer to gather their feedback on the program, including their reflections on diversity and inclusion.

Craft explicit goals for summer associate supervisors to provide a consistent experience to all summer associates.

- Develop a written set of expectations regarding the program's professional activities (i.e., the job-related experiences that the firm tries to expose *all* summer associates to by the end of the summer).
- Create a standard evaluation for all summer associates and distribute the written assessment at the end of the summer to each summer associate.

Make strategic interpersonal and work assignments.

- In pairing supervisors with summer associates, select supervisors on the basis of their performance, not their race.
- Resist the temptation to assign summer associates of color only to lawyers of color within the firm.
- Ensure that summer associates of color and white summer associates have similar work experiences and similar opportunities to engage in non-work activities within the firm. This could be accomplished by having centralized assignments or by having periodic check-ins with summer associates to assess the nature of their work assignments, including the flexibility to make adjustments when differences are detected.
- Survey summer associates on the types of assignments they are receiving and to gauge whether they have someone in the firm to turn to for support.

Engage affinity groups in the summer associate experience.

- A firm's affinity groups, internal organizations made up of lawyers of color, women, and other self-identified cohorts, should mentor summer associates of color.
- Opportunities for conversations on firm culture, professionalism, and career path development should be included in formal affinity group programming.

Stay alert to personal interactions to ensure a supportive environment.

Firm leadership and senior associates may need additional guidance on the most effective and helpful ways to engage with associates of color. Part of the work involves exercising empathy and imagining what the experience might be like for people of color in their particular law firm environment. Finding ways to engage people of color to elicit their views, hear their perspectives, and engage in meaningful dialogue about their

experience can also help a law firm make the neces-
sary changes to build a more supportive environment.
What follows are some recommendations on ways to
accomplish that goal:

*Invite feedback from associates of color by asking
simple, open-ended questions about their experiences
at the firm.*

- Start with the basics: "How is it going?"
- "We understand that you are billing the hours
  that you need to bill, but are you satisfied with
  the work that you are getting?"
- "Are you feeling a sense of gratification from
  your work? From the environment? What
  could we do better?"

*Invite feedback from associates of color on the chal-
lenges of fitting in.*

- Recognizing that people of color may worry
  about authenticity in the workplace, a super-

visor might ask: "Do you feel that you can bring your whole self to work?"

- "We understand that things important to you in your personal life have a bearing on your experience in the firm. Are you able to be yourself here?"

Ask senior associates and partners questions to reinforce diversity and inclusion goals.

- "Are you supervising the assignments lawyers of color are receiving?"
- "Are you making yourself available for feedback conversations?"
- "Do you know the associate's goals and aspirations?"
- "Is the associate in the right practice?"
- "Within the practice, who would be the best partner to shepherd this associate's career?"
- "What steps are you taking to give the associate of color opportunities to stretch him- or herself?"

Make feedback consistent, transparent, and helpful.

- Supervisors must be reminded that no one comes into a firm as a full-fledged attorney and that all of us need some guidance in the development of our professional brand. That attitude—that great lawyers are made and not born—must be top of mind for those supervising and managing young associates.
- Senior associates and partners are often consciously or unconsciously biased when it comes to associates of color. In addition, they often maintain uninformed perceptions of people of other races and ethnicities. Partners and associates should be coached to be alert for such biases in the feedback and guidance they give to associates of color.
- Feedback should be timely and contemporaneous with work so that associates of color can make adjustments based on those suggestions.

- The form of the feedback should be consistent. Supervisors should not be harder or softer on lawyers of color.

- Supervisors should avoid casually disparaging the work of lawyers of color or commenting about mistakes in a wider setting, recognizing that even small errors will be held against lawyers of color in ways that are not typically experienced by their equally mistake-prone white colleagues.

- An appropriately trained member of the HR or talent development staff should be tasked with reviewing feedback reports and evaluations to search for biases, trends in feedback, "unfair graders," and supervisors who provide a lack of actionable feedback. An example of bias would be reviewers habitually describing women who exhibit a certain behavior as "aggressive" while describing men exhibiting the same behavior as "go-getters."

In the same sense, associates of color who act similarly are often viewed as "cocky" or "overconfident."

Recognize the unique role affinity groups can and should play.

Affinity groups can provide informal feedback and assistance to their membership. Within law firms, they often play critical roles in supporting lawyers and law students of color. A firm can make strides in shaping its culture by asking specifically for the help and ideas of affinity groups and by meeting routinely with them to get feedback on how it is doing and what steps it can take to build a more supportive environment.

In addition, firms can ask affinity groups to take on individual mentoring roles with early career associates of color. Affinity groups can offer a critical safe place to seek and deliver feedback. Group members can help associates of color with a range of granular issues, from making sense of the assignment process, to decoding feedback from the assigning attorneys, to

helping an associate to understand that, despite assur-
ances, everything may not be okay if they are getting
assigned less work than their white counterparts.

*Empower affinity groups to play a critical decod-
ing role.*

- A firm's affinity groups can work directly with
  individual associates of color to help them
  navigate the specific culture of the firm, shar-
  ing insights about personalities and politics
  within the firm that are often otherwise un-
  spoken.
- Affinity groups can provide helpful guidance
  about the nuances that inform the judgments
  about and impressions of an associate. How
  an associate dresses, how he engages in de-
  bate or conveys disagreement, and what he
  chooses to share about his personal life are all
  matters that, in addition to his work product,
  factor into his personal brand. Affinity groups
  can help new associates of color become more

183

aware of how they are perceived so that they can make conscious choices about shaping their image.

· Affinity groups should also help young associates with the "30,000-foot view," encouraging associates of color not to just bill a lot of hours, but to actively seek out different types of matters and transactions to broaden their exposure to different areas of the practice.

LAW SCHOOLS

Law students—and particularly law students of color—often entered law school believing that advancement inevitably flows from working hard and applying themselves. They then assume that making progress in a professional setting means more of the same: continuing to perform in the manner that has helped them advance academically. But professional success has additional demands. Everyone at a large law firm is expected to produce at a very high level. Success in a firm environment takes more.

At a minimum, advancement at a law firm is premised on relationship building (identifying and cultivating mentors and sponsors) and positioning oneself to take on new challenges. Law schools often claim to be in the business of preparing the next generation of leaders in law. But to do so means helping law students to understand what success looks like and preparing law students of color to hit the ground running when they work as summer associates and when they begin work as full-time associates. This means helping them understand how law firms do business. What follows are steps that law schools can take:

Prepare students of color to understand how law firms operate.

Explain that law firms are businesses with financial goals and metrics of success.

- Help students learn to identify the growth areas of a firm and how they can contribute to the firm's success in those areas.

- Explain the keys to success at a law firm, which include not only hitting billable-hour targets but also volunteering for tasks *and* being a thought partner and problem-solver.
- Offer explicit instruction, especially to law students of color, about the role of an associate at a law firm, which is to support the work of senior attorneys and partners as effectively as possible. Law schools can prepare students of color by offering role-playing and trainings that help them understand and act on the following principles:
- Associates work directly for senior associates or partners, and success depends on knowing the priorities of those individuals.
- New lawyers will build trust—as well as their personal brand—by helping their supervisors meet goals and by exceeding their supervisors' expectations.
- Understanding and monitoring the supervisors' and senior associates' expectations will

help the professional relationships develop on both ends.

- Clients are the ultimate audience, and their expectations are high.
- The quality of work must be perfect.
- Assignments do not stop when a memo or brief is turned in. Associates are expected to do the work assigned and think three steps ahead, anticipating next steps and problems that could arise.
- Some feedback is implicit rather than explicit. If you are not getting new work assignments, there is a problem.
- Top-notch work will lead to involvement in the high-stakes matters outside of the firm's regular assignment system.
- Face time is important, during the workday and at the firm's social events.
- Age matters: the age demographic of the partnership sets the standard for how associates and partners interact with one

187

another. Pay attention to what matters to the partners—physical presence in the office, dress codes, level of interaction—to meet their expectations.

- Volunteer for difficult tasks.
- Seek out mentors and sponsors for help navigating the various levels of the profession.
- Doing a good job on assignments is a starting point, not a destination.
- Build a personal and professional brand from the first day in a firm, as a summer associate or entry-level lawyer.

Offer explicit instruction on the importance of diversity and inclusion for all law students and all lawyers.

Law schools must teach that diversity and inclusion are the responsibility of everyone in the school and in the profession, not simply people of color. To that end, they should do the following:

- Use orientation programs to teach all students about the importance of diversity and how the profession benefits as a whole from a diversity of viewpoints.
- Sponsor discussions about racial identity, including critically examining the privileges that attend whiteness in this country.
- Encourage law professors to raise and address issues of marginalization in their courses so that students learn to identify these issues as part of the practice of being an effective lawyer.
- Prepare students for a profession in which clients expect to see diverse teams, and in which lawyers likewise expect to work with a wide range of people—whether they are judges, opposing counsels, colleagues, or clients.
- Law schools should teach all law students the fundamentals of being a good ally to marginalized groups, including:

- *Teaching law students to raise questions or to articulate concern when they hear or witness evidence of racism or other forms of discrimination.*
- *Teaching them ways to point out the negative impact of disparaging comments about certain groups or individuals of color.*

While the recommendations in this playbook cannot guarantee a diverse and inclusive workplace, they do provide demonstrable and measureable ways to track the progress of law firms in these vital areas.

ACKNOWLEDGMENTS

I WOULD LIKE TO ACKNOWLEDGE A NUMBER OF PEOPLE who have made this publication possible. I would like to thank the law firm partners who have demonstrated their ongoing commitment to diversity in our profession, Debo P. Adegbile, Lisa Davis, Damaris Hernández, and Ted Wells. In addition, I would like to thank the diversity professionals who not only gave their time, but helped us think through the challenges of this type of book and gave thoughtful comments throughout the publication process.

At NYU School of Law, our own new assistant dean for diversity and inclusion, Lindsay Kendrick, was willing to take time out to offer suggestions and insights, for which I am very grateful. The team at the Center on Race, Inequality, and the Law—Danisha Edwards, Sarah Hamilton-Jiang, Vincent Southerland, and Professor Deborah Archer—all made substantial contributions to this work. Kim Taylor-Thompson also made suggestions, comments, and edits that helped move the project along. I especially want to thank zakia henderson-brown and my dear friend Diane Wachtell, whose creativity, great editing, and commitment to social and racial justice have not only helped advance this work, but have animated all that is good about The New Press.

Finally, I want to thank the staff, students, and faculty of the NYU School of Law, who have supported my work and the work of the Center in these challenging times.

ABOUT THE AUTHORS

Debo P. Adegbile is a partner at Wilmer Cutler Pickering Hale and Dorr and co-chair of the firm's Anti-Discrimination Practice.

Lisa Davis is a partner in the Entertainment Group at Frankfurt Kurnit Klein & Selz.

Damaris Hernández is the first Latina partner in Cravath, Swaine & Moore's litigation department.

Ted Wells is a partner at Paul, Weiss, Rifkind, Wharton & Garrison and co-chair of the firm's litigation department.

Anthony C. Thompson is a professor and faculty director of the Center on Race, Inequality, and the Law at New York University School of Law, author of *Releasing Prisoners, Redeeming Communities* and *Dangerous Leaders*, and co-author of *A Perilous Path* (The New Press).

They all live in New York.

**Also from the New York University School of
Law Center on Race, Inequality, and the Law**

*A Perilous Path: Talking Race,
Inequality, and the Law*
Sherrilyn Ifill, Loretta Lynch, Bryan Stevenson,
and Anthony C. Thompson

A no-holds-barred, red-hot discussion of race
in America today from some of the leading
names in the field
Available in hardcover and ebook

PUBLISHING IN THE
PUBLIC INTEREST

Thank you for reading this book published by The New Press. The New Press is a nonprofit, public interest publisher. New Press books and authors play a crucial role in sparking conversations about the key political and social issues of our day.

We hope you enjoyed this book and that you will stay in touch with The New Press. Here are a few ways to stay up to date with our books, events, and the issues we cover:

- Sign up at www.thenewpress.com/subscribe to receive updates on New Press authors and issues and to be notified about local events
- Like us on Facebook: www.facebook.com/newpressbooks
- Follow us on Twitter: www.twitter.com/thenewpress

Please consider buying New Press books for yourself; for friends and family; or to donate to schools, libraries, community centers, prison libraries, and other organizations involved with the issues our authors write about.

The New Press is a 501(c)(3) nonprofit organization. You can also support our work with a tax-deductible gift by visiting www.thenewpress.com/donate.